Gingerbread Houses

Baking & Building Memories

NONNIE CARGAS

CR

Krause Publications
700 East State St., Iola, WI 54990-0001
Telephone (715) 445-2214
www.krause.com

Please call or write for our free catalog of publications. Our toll-free number to place an order or obtain a free catalog is 800-258-0929 or please use our regular business telephone 715-445-2214 for editorial comment and further information.

Library of Congress Catalog Number 99-61262
ISBN 0-87341-711-9

Printed in the United States of America

Dedication

This book is dedicated to my parents: Millie Rieder Cargas, who taught me to love crafts at an early age, and Harry James Cargas, who, as far as I know, never did a craft in his lifetime, but who always knew that I would write books in mine. May God bless them both.

Acknowledgments

I would like to thank all of my friends, and even acquaintances, from the world of cake decorating in general, and from the I.C.E.S. in particular, for all of the hints, tips, ideas, and pictures they generously shared with me throughout the writing of this book. They are too numerous to mention by name.

Thank you to Seiche Sanders, Paul Kennedy, and Amy Tincher-Durik at Krause Publications for offering me the book contract and assisting with the manuscript.

Many thanks to Jaci Salisbury, teacher, friend, and expert cake decorator, who helped with everything from sharing ideas and judging a contest, to hosting a charity event. If any of my readers live within driving distance from Washington, D.C., consider taking a class at her fabulous school, Artistry With Cake (see Resources, page 183).

Also, many thanks to my baker, Donna Beth Joy Shapiro, owner of the world's sweetest business, The Old Waverly Tea Room. Using my recipe and patterns, and her professional equipment and expertise, she baked most of the gingerbread pieces for the structures in this book. She did a beautiful job, and if you live in the Baltimore area you must check out her extraordinary cookies and cakes. They are not only gorgeous and delicious, some of them are even technologically advanced!

To George Gibbs, my photographer, thanks are not enough. His interest, professionalism, and excellent photography skills have added to the quality of this book immeasurably. I will always be grateful.

Finally, and most sincerely, thanks to my family, Kostas, Theo, and Daphne Lyketsos. They steadfastly supported and encouraged my work. Although they went hungry at times, they left my gingerbread houses intact. My appreciation and love are endless.

Table of Contents

Introduction

In a span of about ten years I have come all the way from making my first gingerbread house to writing a book about the craft. The idea of a book certainly wasn't in my head that cold winter's day when I decided to try my first gingerbread project, but as I reflect on it now, the path was relatively straightforward from dawning interest to completed manuscript. Here's how it happened.

When we were first married, my husband used to work long hours, so I would look for projects to keep myself busy. While shopping at the mall one Christmas break, on a whim, I purchased a cast-iron gingerbread mold from Williams Sonoma. The pan was gorgeous, and I still have it in pristine condition, but the tiny little gingerbread house I made with it was not. Fortunately, I didn't know it at the time. We lived in one of the rowhouses that Baltimore is famous for, and, one by one, I dragged my neighbors down to ours on the end to marvel at my mini-masterpiece.

They admired it too, although I now know they were just being polite. It was enough to keep my ego and my interest going, though, and I continued to make gingerbread houses every year. I also began collecting magazine articles and books on gingerbread; I found some very beautiful volumes, but none with the assortment of ideas for which I was looking. This is when the thought crossed my mind that maybe there was a book that still needed to be written.

Soon I had children, two in a row, and I wanted to develop a real hobby, as well as learn how to decorate their birthday cakes. I began to take cake decorating lessons at a local cake store. I also took any gingerbread classes I could find, and my skills slowly began to improve. Encouraged by progress, I became obsessed with cake decorating. I

couldn't get enough of it, so I joined I.C.E.S.—the International Cake Exploration Societe—and made tons of friends (at both my local chapter and the annual international convention). From there I became the Children's Editor for *American Cake Decorating Magazine* under the esteemed team of Bob and Addie Harte. However, every time I came across an idea for a gingerbread house, I squirreled it away for the book I might one day write.

At some point during those years I even got around to writing a book proposal for a gingerbread book. At about ten pages long, it outlined my plan for prospective publishers. Then I showed it to a professional writer acquaintance of mine for evaluation. She recommended major revision, and that was just for the proposal! Forget it, I thought. I had two toddlers at home and more than enough to keep me busy. Still, my interest in the craft of gingerbread continued unabated.

Time went by and my toddlers grew into preschoolers. One day I stumbled across the old book proposal in my desk drawer. I made

some changes and sent it off. I remember mailing it out on a Friday, then hopping on a plane to St. Louis to take my children to see their grandparents. By the time I came home the following Monday there was a message from Krause Publications on my answering machine. There were still a few months of questions and answers back and forth between us, but the following spring I was offered a contract.

During negotiations I told the Acquisitions Editor, Paul Kennedy, that at that time every single title on the non-fiction bestseller's list had a colon in the title. Naturally, I wanted to put a colon in the title of my book. He suggested that if I added sex and murder to the concoction, we'd have a hit. Well, I never managed to add sex or murder to the mix, but, although it doesn't show it on the cover, I did get a colon in the title. I was on my way.

However, a little over three months after I got the book contract my dad died unexpectedly. He was the author of thirty-two books himself, and he always told me I could, should, and would write books myself. He was very proud of me, but I never got the chance to tell him that the book was dedicated to him and my mom. Then a few weeks later my friend Jennifer Rumberg Van Scoter

died. She, too, was an enthusiastic supporter of this project, and she put me in touch with another Jennifer Van Scoter, her sister-in-law, who contributed to this book. The story of its development cannot be told without including my dad and Jenny's untimely passings.

After those deep blows, I tried to slosh my way through the work, but it took me several months to get back up to speed. Now here I am writing the Introduction and putting together the finishing touches.

What is my reason for telling you this story? It is for all of those people, scores of crafters, cake-decorators, and friends, who have told me along the way that they, too, have a book they want to write. Some are too busy, some don't know how to approach it, some are just day-dreaming, and some are really going to do it one day. Here's how I did it, for better or worse. May it inspire you to write your book. And to all gingerbreaders, potential authors or not, happy decorating.

Nonnie Cargas

nonnie@chesint.net

6

Chapter 1

Materials and Supplies

Shopping for gingerbread supplies can be a great deal of fun, but you'll soon find that it can be expensive as well. Experienced gingerbread professionals know that this is not a poor person's hobby (is anything?), but there are things you can do to keep the costs down. First, begin by gathering the essentials. Ingredients for the gingerbread dough and royal icing are really the only things you have to have, as long as your kitchen has the most basic rolling pin, pans, knives, and oven. Many cute little mail-order gingerbread houses even come on bases made of gingerbread, so technically you don't even have to have a base on which to put your house. However, the vast majority of bakers do use them, so I'm listing a sturdy base as a must-have item. Candy isn't even essential: There have been many an adorable gingerbread house done with only beautifully baked gingerbread pieces and cleverly applied royal icing. Again, though, most people do use sweets, so they are listed as essentials as well.

Next, look over the list of highly recommended supplies. Unless you're trying to save every penny possible, you probably want to have these things in your possession. They are all items people who make a great deal of gingerbread own and use regularly.

Finally, leaf through Chapter 3, Decorating Information, Inspiration, and Ideas, to see what other special touches you want to give your gingerbread house; then shop accordingly.

 *Tip: Assemble your ingredients and plan your project before you begin!*

One question that came up repeatedly in my gingerbread classes was "What is the shelf life of molasses?" It is 24 months.

Checklist

Items You Must Have:

Candy, cookies, and other edible decorations (including ready-made sugar decorations)

Ingredients for the gingerbread dough (or purchase store-bought, pre-baked pieces)

____ flour	____vegetable shortening (good quality)
____sugar	____baking powder
____unsulphered molasses	____salt
____ground ginger	____cinnamon

Ingredients for royal icing

____powdered sugar	____meringue powder

____Pattern (or cutters or mold)
____Sturdy base

Very Useful Items:

____Cake decorating bags

____Cookie rack for cooling pieces

____Couplers and tips

____Drying table

____Foil covering for base

____Heavy-duty stand mixer

____Marble rolling pin

____Parchment paper

____Paste colors to color icing (or dough)

____Shiny, heavy-gauge aluminum pans

____Small, angled spatula used to spread the icing

____Toothpicks

____Turntable for turning the house while decorating

____X-acto knife

____Yard sticks, rulers, or special rubber bands for your rolling pin to help ensure even dough thickness

Some of the items listed are discussed in detail on pages 9-14 (in the order they appear in this list).

Ready-made Sugar Decorations

In recent years, cake outlets have had an explosion of the available sugar decorations. Every season dozens of clever, new creations are offered to customers. The decorations are usually mass-produced in royal icing and could be easily imitated at home with common decorating tips. However, most of them are inexpensive, so I find that buying them is money well spent.

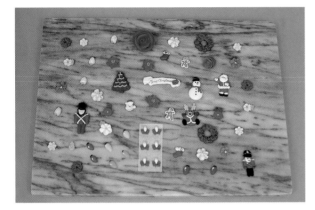

Cake stores carry tons of ready-made sugar decorations.

Copying Patterns

The easiest way to copy any pattern, including the ones in this book, is to take them to a copying machine. After copying, cut out the pieces. You can either use these cut-outs as your pattern or trace around them on thin cardboard for a more permanent pattern. Those made from paper will likely be thrown away after one use, but those made of cardboard can be saved year after year in plastic bags. (Note: They do get greasy after being laid down on the gingerbread dough.)

I usually make a paper pattern that I throw away when I'm done. That's because I usually don't make the same house year after year; I like to switch around. Unless you are absolutely sure you're going to make the same house in the future, or you have limited access to a copying machine, I recommend you save yourself an extra step and just use a paper pattern. And, if a copying machine is impossible to come by, good old-fashioned tracing paper works just fine, too.

 TIP: *Cereal boxes, with their waxy fronts, make excellent cardboard for gingerbread patterns. File folders also work well.*

 TIP: *If the pattern sticks to the gingerbread, spray it lightly with non-stick cooking spray.*

Cutters

Cutters usually come in small sizes. They are very convenient for making a series of small houses because you can cut and bake a number of roofs and walls at the same time.

Plastic cutters should only be used on gingerbread dough before baking, because hot dough can melt them.

Molds

Gingerbread molds come in a variety of forms, from extremely durable cast-iron pans to bakeable plastic mini molds (see page 49). Using them shortens the amount of time you need for rolling and cutting the dough. The actual baking time is sometimes longer, however, because some molds only cast half of a gingerbread house at a time, so you have to do it twice. Molds leave lovely imprints in the dough that you can leave as they are or trace with royal icing to make beautiful outlines.

Gingerbread molds are a convenient way to ensure a well-shaped structure.

Cake Boards and Bases

Any sturdy board makes a good gingerbread board, as long as you remember that gingerbread houses are heavy when fully assembled and decorated. Shown in the picture from left to right: Particle board (as well as plywood, not shown) is available at any lumberyard. Foamboard, often called foamcore, is available at large craft centers. Both cake drums and boards can be found at cake decorating stores and through mail order companies.

Most gingerbread houses are heavy and require sturdy boards beneath them.

If you are using cake boards, be sure to use at least three and stagger them so that the lines don't all run in the same direction. They are much stronger when staggered.

Quick Fact: Many American families make it a tradition to create their gingerbread house the day or weekend after Thanksgiving.

Decorating Bags

The three types of decorating bags are reusable plastic, disposable plastic, and disposable parchment paper. Each has its own advantages, and it is up to you to discover which one you like best.

How to use a coupler: First, push the large part of the coupler down into the end of your decorating bag. With scissors, trim the bag 1/4" or more below the grooves of the coupler. (Trim too high and the bag is ruined.) Attach the desired tip on the outside of the bag and secure with the coupler ring. To change tips, unscrew the ring, attach the desired tip, and screw the ring back on.

Reusable plastic is the modern version of the old cloth decorating bag. It is the least expensive of the options because it can be used time and time again. It is also easy to handle, due to its thin, flexible material. However, it carries with it one caveat: it can only be used with royal icing. Period. Don't be tempted to use an old buttercream bag if you are a cake decorator. The residual grease from the buttercream will break down the royal icing, and your house will fall apart. Buy a new bag and mark it clearly with a permanent marker, "Royal Icing Only."

Disposable plastic bags are the easiest and most convenient to use, but they can also be the most expensive if you use a lot of colors (and therefore need a lot of bags), or you are making a large number of gingerbread houses (and keep throwing away disposables day after day). However, if you only make one house a year, and use only white icing at that, buying one disposable plastic bag a year is actually the cheapest way to go (and some penny pinchers have been known to even wash these out).

Parchment paper decorating bags are consistently cheap *and* disposable. Buy a package once and it will last you a long, long time. They are also good if you like to use a wide variety of colors when you decorate, because they are so inexpensive. Many decorators even cut them in half to make small bags when using only small amounts of one color.

How to Fold a Parchment Bag

1 *Place parchment triangle in front of you with the right angle corner facing up.*

2 *Curve the outside corner inward until it reaches the middle. A tip should form at the bottom of the parchment paper.*

3 *Curve the opposite corner inward in the same way to form the bag. Fold the top peaks down, inside of the decorating bag. Tape the seams, if desired. (Most professional chefs don't use tape, but I always do.)*

My husband doesn't think I should endorse a product unless I get some tangible benefit from it, like a lifetime supply of decorating bags or a trip to Tahiti. However, I used a roll of Hygo decorating bags throughout the writing of this book and I came to rely on them. The first time I saw them was at a cake decorating convention in St. Paul, Minnesota, where I snapped up a roll. I found them to be fast, convenient, and ready-to-use, and I've relied on them ever since. They are also strong; out of the dozens and dozens I used, not a single one ever split apart. To find out more about them, contact Hygo (see Resources, page 184).

Poor Person's Drying Table

A poor person's drying table is made with toothpicks inserted into Styrofoam. It works just as well as the nail and wood drying tables used by professional artists. Its purpose is to hold gingerbread pieces up so that the icing on every side dries evenly and unobstructed. I made it specifically to dry the gingerbread people for the World project in this book, but it was so useful that I used it for many other items as well.

This drying table is the bargain version of a common artist's tool.

Covering the Base

You do not have to cover your base, especially if you are using an attractive board or a tray. However, if you do choose to cover it, it must be with a foil-type material. Anything made of cloth will absorb moisture from the icing and leave an unfortunate ring around your project.

Specialty foils add pizzazz to any project.

The average kitchen aluminum foil works fine, but you can add some pizzazz with specialty foils, like those shown here, which come in a variety of colors. They are sold at cake decorating stores for the serious decorator at about $10 a roll. However, most shops also sell it by the foot from behind the counter, so be sure to ask. That way you can buy two to three feet in your favorite color for a fraction of the cost of buying a whole roll.

Heavy-duty Stand Mixer

Heavy-duty stand mixers, often referred to as Kitchen Aids because of the best-selling brand name, are excellent for both mixing gingerbread and making royal icing. Real workhorses in the kitchen, these mixers can handle thick doughs with ease, as well as the long running time royal icing sometimes requires. Small hand-held mixers, on the other hand, sometimes have difficulty with thick dough and long running times. When especially overworked, the motors of these mixers burn out and the entire appliance must be replaced. If you plan on making a good deal of gingerbread, consider investing in a good-quality heavy-duty mixer.

Rolling Pins

Four types of rolling pins are pictured here, from the left: wooden, serrated, non-stick, and marble. The basic wooden rolling pin that most people own is fine. I used one for many years with good results. The serrated rolling pin is used on anything on

A wide variety of rolling pins is available at cooking and cake decorating stores.

which you want lines; I frequently used it to make shutters out of fondant. The dark-colored, non-stick rolling pin is lightweight and easy to wield, but you need to make up for its lack of weight by paying careful attention to the amount of pressure you exert. The marble rolling pin is the best. Its smooth surface and heavy weight are great for rolling out a smooth, even dough. Since I purchased my marble rolling pin, it's the only one I use for gingerbread.

Parchment Paper

Flat parchment paper, sometimes called baking paper, is useful to gingerbreaders in a number of situations. If, for some reason, you have to move your pieces from the place where you're cutting them out to the pan on which they'll be baking, cut them out on parchment paper and then move the whole ensemble. That way there is no distortion. Parchment paper also keeps your baking sheets clean; the dough doesn't touch them and the sheets don't need to be sprayed with oil. They are also reusable and can be removed quickly from a hot pan (again, with no distortion). If you are trying to do a perfect job, you can never go wrong with parchment paper.

The only drawback, and indeed the reason that I don't use it often, is that it's expensive. I cut my pieces directly on the baking sheet that I'm using, so parchment paper is not essential. Professional pastry chefs bypass this dilemma altogether by using fabulous industrial-quality, industrial-priced reusable baking mats called Silpats. They lie down in the pan like parchment paper, encourage very even baking, and can be used over and over. I hear they're great, but again, definitely not essential.

Paste Colors

Paste colors are thick food colors that add brilliant hues to icings and doughs without adding a great deal of moisture (thus distorting the recipe). They are available at cake decorating stores and mail order companies in dozens of beautiful shades. Some decorators have favorite brands they like to stick with, but I think they're all great.

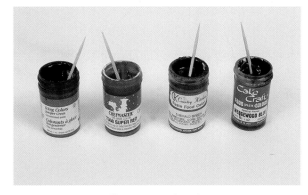

Decorators usually use toothpicks for scooping paste colors.

Pans

Shiny, heavy-gauge aluminum pans are the best choice for baking gingerbread. Dark pans tend to absorb too much oven heat and can overbrown your gingerbread. If you only have dark sheets, or your shiny sheets are thin, try lining them with aluminum foil for a more even distribution of heat (thus a more even browning).

All cookies brown best on shiny, heavy-gauge aluminum pans.

Insulated pans work well for baking gingerbread, but they extend the baking time by quite a bit. Be prepared to leave the gingerbread in the oven for one-and-a-half to two times as long as the recipe suggests.

Note that most of the pieces for the houses in this book were baked in a professional oven with professional pans and pan liners, which resulted in very even browning. This quality is more difficult to achieve in a conventional household oven, so don't be discouraged if you get a little more browning at the edges of your pieces; it's to be expected.

Angled Spatulas and Palette Knives

Angled spatulas are used to spread royal icing snow easily and accurately. Other utensils can be used in place of them, but they don't have the same maneuverability, and the icing doesn't end up looking quite as good.

Small palette knives from an art store are useful, too. They can spread snow in small spaces, nudge a decoration back into place, or remove tiny imperfections without disturbing the area around them. Once I started using palette knives, I found them indispensable.

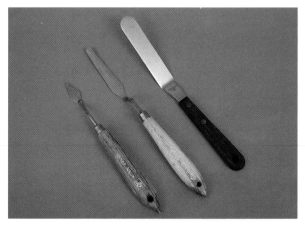

Angled spatulas and palette knives are a useful addition to your decorating collection.

Icing is spread both easily and artfully with an angled spatula.

Chapter 2

The Basics

I must begin this section by telling you, in all truth, that I have never had a gingerbread house collapse. I have not even had one sag after assembly. If anything, they have gotten stiffer and staler over time, and I think that using the right recipes and techniques, you should expect the same. However, while doing extensive research for this book, I spoke with a number of teachers and ran across many books and magazine articles that essentially expected the gingerbread to be too weak to support itself. They began by teaching their students how to make internal support structures, even for small houses. Not only do I find this extra work to be unnecessary, I think that the additional labor takes the joy out of putting the houses together. I ran across this mindset so many times, in fact, that I was beginning to think that I was the only one in America who actually expected her gingerbread houses to stand. That is, until I received a letter from Sheila Miller in York, Pennsylvania, who wrote, "If the correct recipe is used, the corners of walls can be angled using an electric router." I laughed out loud when I read that sentence, not only because it was great idea, but also to know that I was not alone in my approach to gingerbread.

This is not to say, unfortunately, that gingerbread houses last forever. Indeed, most do not make it to the one-year point in perfect shape, but that is because the royal icing breaks down, not the gingerbread. Only little bits usually break at first, though, so repairs can definitely be made to spruce the

houses up if that is what you want to do. I, however, am a firm believer in *eating* the gingerbread. After all, the beauty of it is that it is an edible art! If the walls weren't made to be eaten, they could just as easily be made out of plywood! Make a ceramic holiday house and save it, make a wooden doll house and save it, but if you make a gingerbread house, you should eat it! (Now with that small tirade out of my system, if you are absolutely determined to save your house, despite my best arguments to the contrary, see pages 127 and 128.)

The two most important things I want to teach you about gingerbread are how to bake sturdy, crisp gingerbread pieces and how to make thick, stiff royal icing. If you can do these two things, I can guarantee you that your house will not collapse. The icing recipe is pretty basic, and will be similar almost anywhere you find it, but there is a wide variation in gingerbread doughs. I have tried dozens, and this one is by far the best I've used.

TIP: I recommend dividing your gingerbread project into two days: the first for baking, the second for assembling and decorating. Otherwise, the scope of the project can get out of hand. If you divide it in half, all of the baking supplies, pans, and patterns can be cleaned up and put away before the icing and decorating supplies are brought out. Also, you will approach the decorating from a fresher, more relaxed point of view than if you have already done several hours worth of work. A fresher decorator is a better decorator.

Gingerbread

After purchasing your materials and supplies, the first thing you must do is bake the gingerbread with a good, reliable recipe. I have tried many different ones in the decade that I have been baking gingerbread, and this is the best I've worked with. The pliable, easy-to-roll dough produces an extremely sturdy cookie that holds up well when assembled into a house. I also think it is quite delicious. Many people asked me throughout the course of writing this book if I was sick of gingerbread. I may have tired a bit of the royal icing that ended up everywhere (because it's basically just smooth, hard sugar), but I never tired of the gingerbread. Anytime I had leftover pieces, or the odd broken piece, I was secretly delighted. I did not gain weight while writing this book, but I did have to do a lot of extra mall walking!

 TIP: *Do not use a recipe that contains baking soda; the dough stays too soft.*

Gingerbread ingredients can be found in almost every grocery store.

 TIP: *Always preheat the oven 10 to 15 minutes prior to baking the gingerbread.*

Gingerbread Recipe

Yield: Approx. 6-1/2 cups dough (which will make most of the houses in this book)

1 cup good-quality all-vegetable shortening
1 cup sugar
1 tsp. baking powder
1 tsp. salt
1 cup unsulphered molasses (light or dark, the only difference is the shade of brown your gingerbread will be)
1 tsp. ground ginger
1 tsp. cinnamon
5 cups flour
4 Tbs. water

Mix the first seven ingredients on medium speed until well blended. Switch mixer to low speed and add flour and water; continue to mix until dough forms. Roll directly onto cookie sheets and cut pattern pieces. Bake 350 for 10 to 15 minutes.*

Rolling the Dough

The less you move your gingerbread pieces, the more likely they are to retain shape. Therefore, roll the dough directly onto the pan, if possible. If the pan has sides, flip it over and roll the dough directly onto the back of the pan. It can be baked on the back of the pan as well; simply put it in the oven upside down.

 TIP: *To keep the pan from slipping when rolling out the dough, put it on a kitchen towel.*

*This baking guideline is extremely tentative due to the wide variations in people's ovens. Very small pieces may have to be baked for only 5 to 7 minutes, while very large pieces may go 20 minutes or more. And insulated baking sheets, which produce beautiful, evenly browned gingerbread pieces, add even more time. The best thing I can tell you is to keep a close eye on your gingerbread, and when the sides begin to brown slightly, remove from the oven and cool, either on the pans or on wire racks. When cool, check the strength of the pieces. If they are not hard, crisp cookies, put them back on the pan and cook for additional time. (Note: You must wait until the pieces have cooled to check their strength, because they are always soft when warm.)

Another option is to roll the gingerbread out onto parchment paper, which can then be lifted onto the pan. This method works great, but parchment paper is expensive. Professional chefs use mats called Silpats, which work even better because they are heavy and do not slide around when the dough is being rolled out, but they are industrial in both size and price.

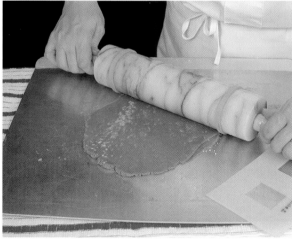

Wooden sticks (top) and rubber bands help to ensure even dough thickness.

Small non-supporting pieces of gingerbread should be approximately 1/4" thick. Larger supporting pieces should be about 3/8" thick. These desired thicknesses can be achieved in a variety of ways.

First, thick rubber bands, specially made for measuring dough, can be put on the ends of your rolling pin. They come in several sizes to lift the pin off of the dough to the desired height. For instance, a 3/8" rubber band will lift the pin enough to produce a 3/8" thick dough. Rolling pin rubber bands can be found at cake decorating stores or mail order companies (see Resources, pages 183-186).

The second way to produce an even thickness is to use two yardsticks (which are usually 1/4" to 3/8" thick) or other straight wooden sticks. (You can also use dowels, but they tend to roll a bit.) Place them on the sides of your dough and roll it flat. The yardsticks prevent the rolling pin from pressing the dough flatter than the desired height.

The most common method of measuring dough is by rolling it carefully while trying to apply even pressure on both ends of the rolling pin and then measuring the results with a ruler. If the dough comes out uneven, reknead it and reroll.

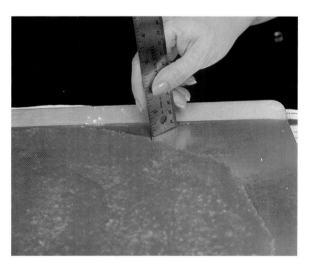

Careful bakers sometimes measure dough with a ruler.

If the sides are close in thickness, place your pattern on the dough. If there is a great deal of variation, though, knead it up into a ball and reroll it. This flexible dough can be easily reworked.

 TIP: Reworking the dough too many times can cause air bubbles. If air bubbles do occur, pop them with a pin immediately after baking and press the cooked pieces down flat with an oven mitt.

If the dough sticks to your rolling pin, there are a number of things you can do:
- *Put a piece of plastic wrap or parchment paper over the dough*
- *Put a pastry cloth around the dough or over the rolling pin*
- *Freeze the rolling pin*
- *Microwave the dough for 30 seconds to soften it*
- *Lightly sprinkle flour onto the dough and even onto the rolling pin itself. (Note: You cannot do this with all gingerbread recipes. In some, the flour will show even after baking, but with this recipe it gets absorbed.)*

The methods I use most often are microwaving and flouring. I find that having a shaker full of flour at my elbow while I am rolling out gingerbread is almost a necessity.

Cut out windows and doors before trimming the sides.

When the dough has been rolled to your satisfaction, cut away the gingerbread with a sharp knife, working from the inside out. By that I mean, if there are any windows or doors in that pattern piece, cut them first. Then trim the sides. This cuts down on any distortion you might get in the pieces. Bake accordingly, cool, and check for hardness (strength). If soft, rebake for several minutes.

 TIP: A good, sharp knife is extremely valuable in keeping the gingerbread edges neat.

Baking the Gingerbread

In general, do not bake little gingerbread pieces with big ones. The little ones will burn while the big ones are still baking. For times and temperature, see the baking guidelines on page 16.

Royal Icing

The second essential element of a sturdy gingerbread house is a stiff royal icing. Consisting of powdered sugar, meringue powder, and water, it functions like cement to hold your house together. And, although I think the number one problem among beginning gingerbreaders is too runny an icing, it is a problem that is easily solved: simply beat the icing longer, perhaps adding a little more powdered sugar.

Royal icing can not be overbeaten. When you first begin mixing it, you will notice that it is a soft white, almost pale yellow color. It is also somewhat runny, like squeezable cheese. However, as you beat it longer you will notice it becoming whiter and stiffer. When you are finished, its consistency will be much closer to smooth peanut butter than to squeezable cheese.

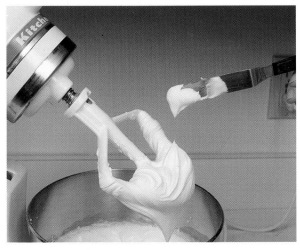

Royal icing is ready when it pulls up into stiff peaks.

TIP: Shortening- and/or butter-based icings are never acceptable substitutes for royal icing; they are simply too soft. (Royal icing dries hard.)

Pull the beaters out of the bowl, or test the icing with a knife. It should pull up into stiff peaks that do not sag. If the icing droops, beat for several more minutes. Remember that the icing cannot be overbeaten, but underbeating it could ruin your house.

A damp towel over the bowl keeps royal icing from hardening.

It is also important to know that this icing crusts over quickly. Therefore, it is essential that your bowl be covered at all times by a tight-fitting lid or a damp towel when you are not directly loading your icing bag. Also, any time you set your icing bag down, the tip should rest in a damp paper towel so that the icing in the hole does not harden. If you forget and the icing in the tip does harden, use a toothpick to dig it out or run it under water for a few seconds to remoisten.

Quick Fact: Although ginger originated in Asia, most of the ginger we currently buy is grown in Jamaica.

Only three ingredients are needed to make hard-drying royal icing: powdered sugar, meringue powder, and warm water.

Quick Fact: *In medieval Europe, gingerbread was an extremely popular item on holidays, market days, saints' days, and fairs. It was sold in pretty shapes and was often gilded and studded with spices. Little cookies called "fair buttons" or "fairings" were sold twenty for a penny.*

Royal Icing Recipe

2 lbs. confectioner's 10x powdered sugar
4 Tbs. meringue powder
10 to 12 Tbs. warm water

In a spotlessly clean, grease-free mixing bowl, combine the sugar and meringue powder. Add the water and beat until the icing forms stiff peaks (about 6 to 8 minutes with a heavy-duty mixer, 10 to 12 minutes with a hand-held mixer).

Keep the icing bowl covered with a damp cloth while it is being used and store it in an airtight container when it is not. (There is no need to refrigerate it.) Rebeat at a low speed, or stir very well with a spoon, before using again.

Note: For successful icing, keep all bowls and utensils completely grease free. Do *not* store leftover icing in margarine, butter, or vegetable oil spread tubs. Residual grease will break down the icing.

 TIP: When you double the royal icing recipe, do not automatically double the water. Use about two-thirds the amount at first, and if it's too dry, add more. For some reason, doubling the water can make it too runny at times, although at other times doubling the water is the right thing to do.

Although you can use a knife to apply royal icing to your gingerbread pieces, I recommend the use of decorating bags. Available in plastic, disposable plastic, or parchment paper, they are easy to use and produce a consistently thick (or thin) bead of icing. Decorating bags can be used with just the end of the bag snipped off or they can be used with a cake decorating tip. If you use a coupler, you can change tips whenever you want without having to change decorating bags. Refer to the discussion of decorating bags on page 10 when deciding which ones to buy.

Preparing the Decorating Bag

If you are not using a variety of tips in your gingerbread decorating, you can simply snip a small hole (1/8") in the end of a decorating bag. If you choose to use just one tip (I recommend the #10), snip off the end of the decorating bag, put the tip inside, and fill with icing. If you want to change tips in the middle of your gingerbread project, use a coupler.

Couplers enable the decorator to change tips without changing decorating bags.

How to Use a Coupler

Place the large part of the coupler inside of the decorating bag. Trim the bag just above the coupler's groove. (Cut it too high and the bag is ruined.) Attach the tip to the outside of the bag and secure with the coupler's ring. Load the bag with icing and proceed to decorate. When a new tip is needed, unscrew the ring, remove the old tip, and attach the new tip with the ring.

Piping

If you have never piped icing from a decorating bag before, you might want to try a few practice squeezes onto a smooth plate before applying directly to your gingerbread house. This icing can be scooped up and deposited right back into the bowl so it

doesn't go to waste, and the several minutes of practice can serve you well down the line.

Folding the end of the decorating bag over your hand makes it easier to fill.

First, load your decorating bag. If you are using a plastic bag, fold it over your hand to open it up. After spooning the icing into the bag, you can actually grab the spoon with the bagged hand to get all of the icing. If you're using a tip with a large opening to do a large job (such as a big #10 because you are assembling the house), fill it with a lot of icing so that you don't have to stop frequently and reload. If you are using a small tip for a small, delicate job (such as a #1 to make lace points), only put a little icing in the bag for ease and maneuverability. Many people, myself included, like to tie the bag with a twist tie after it has been loaded to stop icing from accidentally being squeezed out the wrong end when decorating. Others, especially experienced decorators, find twist ties unnecessary.

TIP: *Remember that you cannot use buttercream bags for royal icing! Residual grease will break down your icing and your house will collapse.*

Decorating Tips

There are hundreds of styles and sizes of decorating tips available to make every type of ruffle, line, and squiggle conceivable. However, there are six basic types useful to gingerbreaders:

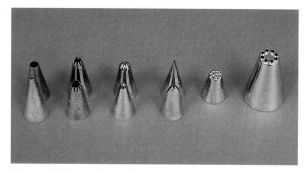

From left to right: plain tips, open star tips, closed star tips, leaf tips, the grass tip, and the wreath tip.

• The plain tips, which have simple round openings, range in number from the tiny #.01 to the large #12. They are used to make dots, balls, and smooth straight lines. If you only buy one tip for your entire gingerbread project, I recommend the #10.
• The open star tips include #13 to #22 and #32. They are used to make star or flower shapes useful for roofs, borders, wreaths, window frames, trim, ornaments, and many other clever applications.
• The closed star tips are #23 to #35 (excluding #32). They are similar to the open star tips, but they create more defined petals, especially if the bag is turned while the petals are being formed.
• The leaf tips come in a variety of sizes: #65 to #70 produce small leaves, #71 to #75 produce large leaves, and #112 to #115 produce extra-large leaves. Tips with notches in the middle produce lovely veins down the centers of the leaves. If you pull the bag forward smoothly when you are squeezing, you make a smooth, straight leaf. If you stall a little bit while you're pulling forward, you can make a nice, rippled leaf. Practice on a plate first—it's easy!
• The grass tip, #233. This clever tip can be used to make grass, fur, pine needles, or any other decoration that needs many fine strands.
• The wreath tip, #235. This tip is perfect for making little green wreaths. Add a small red bow with a #1, #2, or #3, and you're all set to go!

Assembling the House

Because you now know to use a strong, hard gingerbread and good, stiff icing, this part of the project should not be difficult. Keep a variety of glasses or cans close by to prop up the pieces, if necessary, and you will be in good shape.

The first thing you need to do is prepare your board. Any foil you want under your house, or lights you want inside of the house, should be placed now. Also, any curtains, crossbars, or other decorations that are attached to the window from the inside should be placed now.

When your board is ready, decide where you want the house to be located. Most people like it toward the back of the board so that they can create a small scene in the front yard, but you can also consider decorating both the front and the back yards or angling the house from a corner if you're using a rectangular board. With that in mind, attach the back wall first, then the two sides, and then the front. Add the roof (and chimney) last.

Tip: Once your house is built, you can pipe decorative icing to cover uneven joints or cracks.

How to Fix a Broken Piece

A broken piece does not a ruined project make. I once brought pre-baked pieces from my home in Baltimore to my parents' house in St. Louis. My dad found them lying on the kitchen table and ate almost half a wall before he was caught. My mom and I patched the piece with cardboard and royal icing, turned the house to hide the error once it was assembled, and kept my dad far away. No one ever knew.

❶ Apply icing along the break and stick the pieces back together.

❷ Cut a piece of cardboard to cover the break. If the break is such that the strength of the building has been compromised, like on this castle wall, cut the cardboard so that it supports as much of the gingerbread as possible, down to the bottom of the piece.

❸ Ice the cardboard to the gingerbread.

❹ Reinforce the cardboard on every side. Let the icing harden completely before assembling the house.

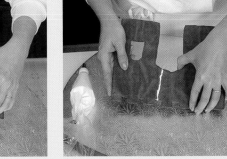

An impression mat pushed too far into the dough created a weak spot where the wall later broke.

❷

❸

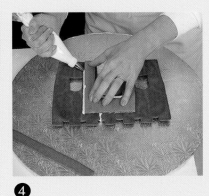
❹

General Instructions for Basic House Assembly

Follow these general guidelines for all gingerbread house construction that consists of four walls and a roof, whether the patterns are from this book or elsewhere.

❶ Pipe a line of icing under the bottom of the back wall and set it directly on the board. Pipe a line of icing in front of the wall and another behind it. Pipe another line of icing up the inside of the wall.

❷ Pipe a line of icing on the cake board where the side wall is to be placed. Attach the side wall. Pipe a line of icing in front of that wall, behind it, up the inside of the wall, and up the outside of it.

❸ Attach the second wall in the same way as the first. Pipe a line of icing up the inside of the back wall, then under the side wall. Attach the side wall to the back wall and pipe icing in front of this wall, behind it, up the inside, and up the outside of it.*

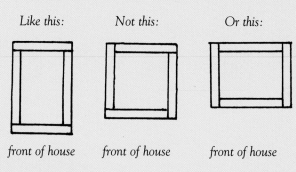

TIP: All of the patterns in this book, except for the graham cracker houses (see page 40) have the walls joined in the same way. The front and back walls are attached to the ends of the side walls.

Like this: Not this: Or this:

front of house   front of house   front of house

❹ Pipe icing up the front of the walls and along the board to support the front wall. Attach the front wall, then reinforce in front, in back, and up the seams. If the house seems fairly sturdy at this point, which it should, proceed with the roof. If not, let the house sit for 15 to 20 minutes so the icing hardens before attaching the roof.

*If you want to create a scene inside of the house, do so now, while three walls are up. Keep in mind that it should have large windows to make this effort worthwhile.

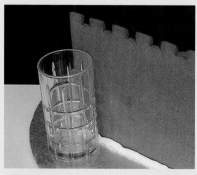

❶ If necessary, use a straight-sided glass or can to support walls.

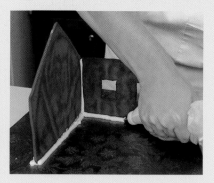

❷

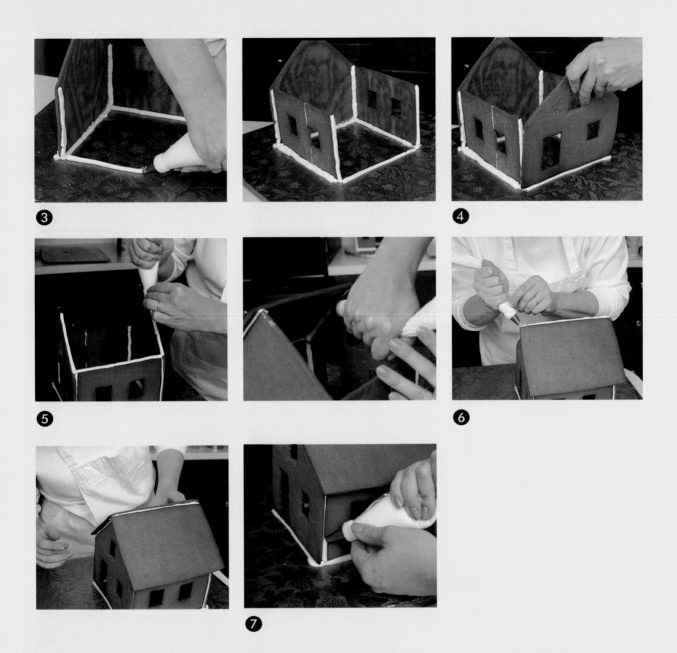

⑤ *Pipe a line of icing along the tops of the walls on half of your house. Place the roof piece on the house. Holding it in place, if necessary, reach inside of the house and reinforce every seam with a thick line of icing.*

⑥ *Pipe a line of icing along the tops of the walls on the other half of your house and along the roof you've already attached. Add the second roof piece. (This piece can not be reinforced from the inside.)*

⑦ *Reinforce every seam on the outside of the house you possibly can. If the roof starts to slide, prop it up with cans or books until set, usually 15 to 30 minutes. (If any more time than that is needed, your icing was too runny to begin with. Try sprinkling the seams with powdered sugar and letting the house set overnight.) Turning on the ceiling fan in my kitchen helps to speed up the drying process for me.*

Now that the serious business of construction has finished, let the joy of decorating begin!

Deciding on Your Style

 TIP: When shopping to create a realistic house, look in the cookie, cereal, and nut aisles for "realistic" building materials.

 TIP: For an example of an all-pastel house, see page 76; for a boldly decorated house, see page 104.

Gingerbread houses usually fall into one of two broad categories: realistic or fantastic. Realistic houses strive for authenticity. Often they attempt to duplicate real homes, down to the very last door hinge. They may have wreaths on the doors and candles in the windows, both made of icing, but they tend not to be covered with huge varieties of candies. Even if the roof is made with sticks of gum or candy melts, they are usually laid down in a pattern that resembles real roof tiles. The same is true of chimneys, sidewalks, and fences: they are created with foods of muted colors like pretzels, nuts, and caramels. This type of house may take a little extra planning before you begin to decorate it, but the result is usually a mini-marvel of ingenuity and craftsmanship.

Fantastic houses may have the basic design of realistic houses, but they are covered in fabulous confections that couldn't possibly exist in the real world. The general rule of thumb here is, the more candy the better! It's very difficult to over-decorate—kitsch and clutter are in. Instead of having

one type of candy cover your roof, have three or four, then trim the edges with one or two more. Enhance the windows and walls with candy where the shutters would be, then add candy where there wouldn't be anything. Fill the yard with trees, bushes, presents, ponds, animals, toys, and all types of candy clutter. This type of house is fun to create, and you can make things up as you go along.

The only angle you might want to plan for when shopping for your candy house is color scheme. Bold and pastel colors tend not to mix well; the bold always overpowers the pastel. Planning for one or the other will help to give your house a unified, cohesive look. Also, consider making a house in only white, silver, and gold for an especially sparkly and attractive holiday house.

Neither realistic nor fantastic gingerbread houses are better than the other. The only difference I've seen is that experienced craftspeople and decorators tend to lean toward the realistic reproductions, and because of the crafters' skill levels, these houses often win the top prizes in competitions. More novice decorators, children, and the general viewing public prefer fantastic, candy-covered dream worlds. If you're trying to attract attention and general acclaim, go for the candy-covered super creations!

 TIP: Watch out for your furry friends when displaying your gingerbread projects—especially cats who can reach high places. Pets have been known to enjoy gingerbread, too!

Quick Fact: Molasses, a common ingredient in most gingerbread recipes, is the liquid that's a leftover when sugar cane juice is boiled down to remove sugar crystals. Light molasses comes from the first boiling of the sugar syrup, dark molasses from the second boiling, and blackstrap molasses is from the third and final boiling. Blackstrap molasses, the thickest, darkest, and most bitter of the three, can sometimes be found in natural food stores.

Decorating the House

Decorating your gingerbread house is the best part of the entire project. (The second best part is the enthusiastic reaction of family and friends.) It is also the most personalized part of the project, with each decorator creating his or her own sugary vision of Home Sweet Home. While one person may fall in love with a realistic, warmly glowing Colonial, the next may want a gold and silver Christmas castle. Children (and many men, too, I've found) almost unanimously prefer the candy- and kitsch-covered Winter Wonderlands—the more "stuff," the better.

Personally, I love it all. From the messy, homemade, first-time candy houses, to the perfect-down-to-the-most-minute-detail prize-winning masterpieces, if it's made of gingerbread, I'm interested in it. Needless to say, I've had a ball writing this book. Not only was I able to see literally hundreds and hundreds of different gingerbread houses, both in pictures and in person, but I was also able to try scores of interesting techniques myself.

It took me two months to make the thirteen houses in this book (not including designing the patterns) and it was all great fun. During that time I was either shopping for candy and cookies, actually assembling and decorating the houses, or managing photo shoots of the finished products. (George, my photographer, and I got a kick out of a beautiful, big-budget food book where the author thanked, among others, a food stylist, a prop stylist, a craftswoman, and an architect. George and I were all of the above, and then some!)

However, I did have a small budget to work with, which enabled me to try many things that may be beyond the home crafter's timetable or budget. I tried to do the legwork for you, to find out what works, and instruct you on how to duplicate those methods. Occasionally I've even included techniques that didn't work so well, or which I found to be difficult. That way, when you're home by yourself, deciding on what you want to try with your project, you can get the opinion of at least one other person (me!). Specific ideas and techniques are covered in Chapter 3, Decorating Information, Inspiration, and Ideas, but what follows here are general guidelines that apply to decorating almost any gingerbread house.

Decorating Guidelines

❶ Decorate the house first (front, back, and side walls), when it is easiest to maneuver your decorating bag. This includes windows, doors, shutters, and other wall decorations.

❷ Decorate the roof next. Always begin at the bottom and work your way up, even if you're not overlapping roof tiles. That way, if there is any unevenness or incongruity when you reach the top it can easily be covered with icing or a candy stick.

❸ Cover the edges with royal icing and add icicles around the outside of the roof. Not only are icicles an excellent way to cover lumpy seams where the walls meet the roof, they're darn cute, too.

❹ Work on your yard quickly, one section at a time. Remember that once royal icing is out in the open air, it crusts very quickly. Therefore, have your bushes, trees, sidewalk materials, etc. ready to be positioned as soon as the icing is spread. A small angled spatula is the best tool for this job.

❷

❸

❹

Chapter 3

Decorating Information, Inspiration, and Ideas

This chapter is like the Home Depot (or Builder's Square, depending upon where you live). There, you can wander up and down the aisles, choosing any number of kitchen and bath products that can be combined in an infinite variety of ways. Here, you can browse through photographs, getting ideas and making plans. Use them in conjunction with an existing pattern for a gingerbread project or as modifications to one of the projects provided in the next chapter. Either way, these ideas are presented to help the do-it-yourselfer make the most of any potential project.

All-Bran

This humble thatched roof was made with Kellogg's All-Bran cereal.

All-Royal House

A gingerbread house made with only gingerbread and royal icing can be both sweet and elegant. It is also easier and less expensive to make than a cookie- and candy-covered creation.

Almonds

Sliced almonds from the bulk-food section of the local grocery store were used to make this "wood tile" roof.

Alphabet Pasta

Small alphabet pasta pieces can be used to make welcome mats, house numbers, retail signs, notices, and street signs. I have always wanted to use them on a sign in front of a church proclaiming the sermon of the week ("This week: Rev. Roy L. Icing on Treating People Gingerly").

Borders, Fences, and Walls

Almost any food item you can think of can be used to make a border, fence, or wall. Pictured here, from front to back, are: ribbon candy, wafer cookies, spearmint leaves, graham crackers, pink mints, and Toblerone chocolate.

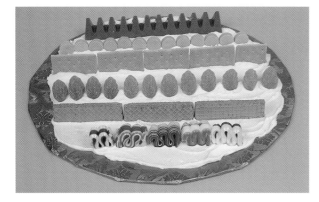

Brown Sugar

Brown sugar makes ideal sand on gingerbread houses. Simply mix each cup of brown sugar with a teaspoon or so of baking powder to keep it from clumping when you're trying to spread it. (See the Southwestern Ranch House on page 96.)

Bullion Cubes

This chimney was made by stacking beef bullion cubes against the house with royal icing. Chicken bullion can be used to attain a lighter color.

Be sure there is no overhang on the roof, as shown here, so the cubes can be stacked right next to the wall of the house. But, if you wish to make an overhang, cut a space into it for the chimney.

Candles

Candles for windows can be purchased at most cake decorating supply stores, but it is also easy to create your own. Make them on waxed paper or parchment paper for easy removal when dry. (Leaving them overnight is best.) Form the candles with a small round tip, such as a #4. Add flames with a smaller tip, such as a #1 or #2. Add leaves with #349, and red berries with a #1 or #2.

Candy Melts

Candy melts come in white, chocolate brown, and a variety of pastel colors and flavors. They can be used for roof tiles and sidewalk stones, or they can be cut in half to make shutters or cute little garden borders.

When melted, candy melts can be used to make anything for which you can find a mold. I used white candy melts with the fence mold to make the picket fence surrounding the Victorian on page 112. The process is easy. Simply estimate the number of candy melts you'll need for your mold and put them in a microwave-safe bowl. Microwave on high, stirring every 30 seconds, until they are completely melted. Spoon into the mold and refrigerate for 10 to 15 minutes or freeze for 5 minutes. Do not let them cool too long in either place, though, or they will crack when they're being removed. To remove, simply pop from mold.

Due to the heat of your hands, candy melt decorations are susceptible to fingerprints. Once they're on the gingerbread display, however, they should be fine; just keep them out of direct sunlight.

Caramels

Caramels are great in any spot where you need squares or bricks, such as chimneys, sidewalks, or walls. They can also be festooned with colorful icing bows to make pretty presents.

To shape caramels into simple forms, like the mailbox in front of the Split-level on page 100, simply push and stroke with warm fingers until the caramel reaches the desired shape.

Chex Mix

Chex Mix cereal (more specifically Wheat Chex) was used to make this cute brown roof.

Coconut

Coconut sprinkled on wet royal icing makes lovely textured snow.

Conical Icing Bushes

These cone-shaped bushes are easy to make. Using a large, open-star tip, such as a #32, make a 1" to 1-1/2" circle of green icing on a cake board. Continue to circle upward in gradually shrinking circles until you have attained the desired height. Sprinkle immediately with decors. These can also be made over gumdrops.

Clear Candy Windows

Clear hard candy, used to make clear "glass" windows, can be difficult to find in stores, so you might want to make your own. If you are trying to achieve a very specific color for your windowpanes, you might want to make your own and tint it the desired color. Candy oil flavorings may be added as well.

Hard Candy Recipe

2 cups granulated sugar
1 cup light corn syrup
1/2 cup water
1/4 tsp. food coloring of choice
Several drops candy oil flavoring (if desired, such as oil of   cinnamon, oil of peppermint, or oil of wintergreen)

Combine sugar, corn syrup, and water in a heavy saucepan. Cook over medium-high heat until boiling, stirring constantly with a wooden spoon to dissolve sugar. This should take about 5 minutes. Avoid splashing mixture on sides of pan. Carefully clip a candy thermometer to the inside of saucepan.

Cook over medium heat, for 20 to 25 minutes, stirring occasionally, until the thermometer registers 290°, soft-crack stage. The mixture should boil at a moderate, steady rate over the entire surface. Remove pan from heat and remove thermometer from pan.

Quickly stir in desired food coloring and flavoring into prepared pan lined with oiled aluminum foil or oiled hard candy molds. Allow to cool.

Coloring Dough

You can vary the gingerbread dough's base color in a number of ways. To make a pale, cream-colored dough, use corn syrup instead of molasses in the basic recipe. To make a pretty light brown dough, use light molasses in the amount indicated in the recipe. To make a beautiful dark brown dough, use dark molasses in the amount indicated. To make a rich, deep, even darker brown dough, use dark molasses and replace 1/2 cup of the flour in the recipe with a 1/2 cup of cocoa powder.

The most effective color to tint your dough is red. Red food coloring in brown gingerbread dough produces a lovely brownish brick red, great for brick houses and red barns. Simply stir a teaspoon of red food coloring into the molasses before adding it to the dough. Then mix, roll, and cut (although be prepared for red hands!). What you see after baking will be a slightly darker version of what you put into the oven unbaked, just like regular dough.

Another option for clearly delineated bold colors is to paint the baked pieces with paste colors. (See Painting with Paste Colors, page 49.)

Color Flow

In color flow, each color must dry completely before another color touches it.

Color flow is a decorating technique that is used to make smooth designs on cookies, pictured here, or hard icing pieces that can be attached to cakes and gingerbread houses when dry. It is also called run sugar, a fitting name because it is simply a matter of adding water to royal icing to make it runny. The only requirement for color flow pieces is that they must be made several days before they are to be attached to the house in order to dry thoroughly.

The instructions for color flow are the same whether you're making them on top of cookies or on top of waxed paper. One nice thing about using waxed paper is that you can put patterns underneath it to trace. I used this technique to make a dozen little animal pieces for my son's birthday cake. I had to make them five days in advance so that they were completely dry and hardened, but when the big day arrived all I had to do was ice the cake, peel the waxed paper off the pieces, and pop them on. They came out great and the kids loved it!

First, either place the cookies on a flat tray or tape waxed paper over patterns on a tray. Next, outline your pieces with regular (unthinned) royal icing. Let harden for 30 minutes or more, until totally dry. In the meantime, prepare your colors.

Divide the royal icing into separate bowls for each color. Tint to the desired shades. (Note that the colors intensify overnight.) Add water, just drops at a time, until the icing achieves the proper state of flow. This occurs when drops of icing, lifted with a spoon and dripped back into the bowl, have blended in completely by the count of six.

Using a separate decorating bag for each color, fill in the sections of the patterns with icing. Let the icing puff up a bit above the outlines because it will shrink when drying. Remember to let each color dry *completely* before adding another color next to it.

There is a color flow powder available at many cake decorating stores that claims to help your color flow pieces, but help them do what, I'm not sure. I have made many color flow pieces both with the product and without, and I find it to be completely unnecessary—there is no difference between the final products.

In summary, color flow is a simple icing technique that is well worth learning. As long as you can make an outline of something (like signs, plaques, and faces), you can create it in color flow.

Creative Color Food Spray

Creative Color brand food decorating spray is like an airbrush in a can. Use it wherever you need a large colored area on baked gingerbread pieces. It is particularly effective on light-colored dough. If your local cake store does not carry it, you can get it through Country Kitchen mail order company (see Resources, page 184).

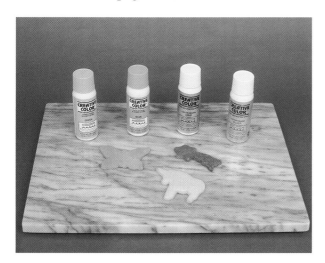

Crushed Candy Ponds

Icy ponds are a breeze to make with crushed hard candy. *If* you cannot find blue hard candy, tint clear hard candy with blue paste color. If you have found them, unwrap the pieces, put them in a baggie, and pound into small chunks with a hammer. (If you're using clear, add blue paste color in between hammer blows.) Pour into a small pile on a foil-lined pan and bake at 350° for 3 to 5 minutes. After the pond has cooled, ice it to the board with a thin layer of white royal icing both under the pond and around it. This not only secures the pond, but also helps it reflect light like real ice.

Crushed Candy Stained Glass Windows

Beautiful stained glass windows are made from hard candy that has been crushed and melted. Simply unwrap the candies*, put each color in a separate baggie, and pound with a hammer into small chunks. Then make small piles of the crushed candy on a foil-lined pan and bake at 350° for 3 to 5 minutes. When cool, ice this "sheet of glass" behind the window opening in your gingerbread.

Some people like to put the crushed candy chucks directly in the window opening for the last 3 to 5 minutes of the gingerbread's baking time. This method works, but it then becomes impossible to rebake the gingerbread if you find it isn't crisp enough. For this reason, I prefer to attach the sheets of "glass" as described above.

Crushed candy stained glass windows look gorgeous when lighted from within, and a small craft light in your gingerbread structure will not melt them. High humidity will, though, so take care on particularly humid days.

*Some of the best hard candies with which to make candy windows are Jolly Ranchers; they retain their bright color even after being melted.

Crystallized Ginger

Crystallized ginger achieves the same look as dried fruit on chimneys, but has the added advantage of being ginger (this being gingerbread, after all). It is available at some large grocery stores and most gourmet food shops.

Curtains

Although they're not edible, I just love the look of curtains made from lace trim inside windows. They never sag or fall off the way some edible decorations can. Just remember to attach them before you put the house together. (The close-ups shown here are from the Fondant Roof Cottage and Victorian, pages 68 and 112, respectively.) For an edible, ruffle-edged curtain, see Lasagna Noodles, page 46.

TIP: *If you make houses with large windows, people will want to peer in, so use curtains or sheet gelatin for cover. Smaller windows don't attract as many peeping toms, so window dressings are optional there.*

Curved Pieces

Some gingerbread crafters, when designing their own projects, are interested in making curved gingerbread pieces for trellises, arched doorways, or domes. These can be made by sliding hot gingerbread directly from the oven onto a curved item like a large can and removed when completely cooled.

Decorating Comb

A decorating comb, usually used on cakes, makes lovely scallops on a roof covered with royal icing.

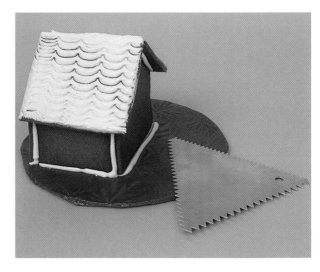

Donut Snowpeople

These donut snowpeople were made with donettes and donut holes, joined together and decorated with royal icing. However, royal icing sometimes has a difficult time adhering to powdered sugar. I had to apply some of the facial features two or three times before they stuck. That's just the nature of the elements! Pretzel sticks were added to the middle donuts as arms.

Dragees

Silver and gold dragees lost popularity when, in 1992, the USDA withheld approval for their consumption. It's not that they're poisonous—even the Poisindex, a computer program used by the state poison-control centers nationwide, lists them as non-toxic—it's just that they haven't been formally studied. The sole producer of dragees in the United States, QA Products of Elk Grove, Illinois, says that the cost of the studies is prohibitive given the small amount of dragees sold*. However, they also say that the amount of precious metal in each dragee (.0003 parts of metal per million, or 310 billionths of each dragee) is minuscule.

The FDA recommends that consumers remove dragees before consumption, but in many European countries there are no such restrictions. For a complete discussion of the dragee dilemma, refer to the May/June 1996 issue of American Cake Decorating Magazine.

Close-up of the Swiss Chalet's dragee-lined roof (see page 106).

Dried Fruit

Dried pineapple and orange were used to make this "stone" chimney.

*Source: Marialisa Calta, "Dragees: What's All the Fuss?," American Cake Decorating Magazine (May/June 1996).

Dusting Powders

Dusting powders are usually used by cake decorators to add color and sheen to their cake decorations, especially gumpaste flowers. However, gingerbreaders can use dusting powders as well when they want to give a lustrous tint or added shine to a particular piece. Gold luster dust was used on the shingles and doormat of the Fondant Roof Cottage on page 68. Also, white pearl dust on the same cottage helped the fondant door shine.

This sign was painted with gold and silver dusting powder mixed with vodka.

Another way to apply dusting powder is to mix it with gin, vodka, or lemon oil (not lemon juice) and paint it on for bold lines, as on the restaurant sign shown here.

All dusting powders are similar to one another, and many people use their different names interchangeably. However, they are technically divided into the following categories:
• Petal dusts (or blossom tints): Shiny, softly colored dusting powders (such as apple green or lemon yellow)
• Luster dust: Iridescent dusting powder
• Sparkle dust: Similar to luster dust, but even more sparkly
• Pearl dust: Pearlescent dusting powder

TIP: When dusting with dry dusting powders, do not use water to clean your paintbrush between colors. Instead, rub your brush on a dry paper towel. When painting with dusting colors that have been mixed with clear liquor or lemon oil, clean the brush with the clear liquor or lemon oil between colors.

Quick Fact: The gingerbread in medieval Europe was made from stale bread, honey, pepper, aniseed, saffron or licorice for color, and ginger. The ingredients were mashed together, shaped or molded, and dried until hard and brittle.

A Joke:
Where do gingerbread people sleep?
Answer:
On cookie sheets!

Edible Glitter

Edible glitter is similar to craft glitter, but it is completely edible. Gingerbreaders often use white to add an extra dimension of sparkle to their royal icing snow, but it comes in a number of other glimmering colors as well. Edible glitter must be sprinkled when royal icing is wet for it to adhere properly. To apply it on icicles or other icing on the sides of a building, blow it gently from a spoon.

Fondant

Fondant is an extremely smooth icing that is often used to cover cakes. Like modeling clay, it is pliable and easy to work with when fresh. Unlike modeling clay, however, it

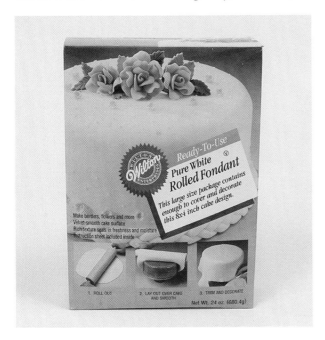

crusts quickly for a stiffer final product. If you can keep in mind the need to work fairly speedily and efficiently when using fondant, you will find it has many useful applications in gingerbreading. Be sure to keep all unused portions tightly wrapped and covered.

Fondant is available ready-made from most cake decorating stores and mail order companies (see Resources, pages 183-186). Some experienced decorators find a particular brand they like and stick with it, but I find them all to be equally good. One exception is white chocolate Choco-pan, which I used when writing this book; it is particularly delicious.

Close-up of the Fondant Roof Cottage's fondant-covered roof (see page 68).

Fondant is used with gingerbread in four ways: draped, impressed, molded, and sculpted.

• **DRAPED:** Rolled fondant that has been draped over the roof of a gingerbread house makes a covering as smooth and pristine as an authentic layer of new-fallen snow. Fondant needs a sticky substance under it in order for it to adhere properly. Therefore, the first thing you need to do is coat the roof with a thin layer of either piping gel or royal icing. Sprinkle a board with powdered sugar. Roll out the fondant, being sure to lift and turn the fondant every second or third pass of the rolling pin so that it doesn't stick to the board. Have a friend lift the board over the roof. Gently slide the fondant from the board onto the house. Smooth the surface of the fondant with your hands, trim the edges, and tuck the ends under the roof.

TIP: You must roll the fondant out onto a board that can be lifted above the roof of the house. Have a friend hold the board while you slide the fondant off.

• **IMPRESSED:** Some people like to impress others, but I like to impress fondant! You will too when you see how easy it is to make realistic house accessories. First, sprinkle your work surface with powdered sugar. Then roll out the fondant and, as stated above, lift and turn the fondant every second or third pass of the rolling pin so that it does not stick to the board. Impress the fondant with the desired pattern. I often use a serrated rolling pin to make slatted shutters or impression mats to create stone walls, brick walls, and wooden doors. Finally, trim down to size. Let the fondant dry for a day or two and then attach it to your house with royal icing.

• **MOLDED:** Molding fondant is a little trickier than impressing it, but the beautiful molds on the market today make it worth the effort for some. First, dust your mold with cornstarch, not powdered sugar (which will cause it to stick). Press the fondant into the mold. Carefully bend the mold to release the fondant and let it dry for a day or two. Attach the molded fondant to your house with royal icing. (Don't be discouraged if it doesn't turn out perfectly the first time; molding fondant takes practice.)

• **SCULPTED:** Sculpting fondant is an excellent way to make cute, edible accessories for your gingerbread projects. Because it is soft, however, it is best for small figurines. Use it as you would modeling clay to form animals, people, and other chunky figures. Keep in mind that two pieces stuck together will not necessarily stay joined. You need to apply either water or gum glue* between the pieces with a paintbrush. Also, these chunky pieces may need to harden over several days rather than overnight.

Close-ups of the A-frame's fondant front door (left) and the Castle's fondant flags (see pages 58 and 80, respectively).

*Gum glue is a homemade concoction consisting of two parts water to one part gum arabic.

Fondant Trees

These fabulous fondant trees make learning to use fondant worth the effort—I just love them. First, coat an ice cream sugar cone with a thin layer of piping gel. Tint a portion of fondant green, roll it out (with powdered sugar, as described above), and wrap it around the cone. Trim off the excess fondant with a knife. Starting at the bottom of the cone, make tiny snips in the fondant with small craft scissors. New cuticle scissors, with their slight upward curve of the tip, work particularly well.

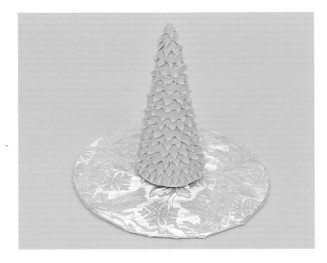

Garlic Press Accessories

A common kitchen garlic press can be used to make delightful decorations and accessories on gingerbread. Simply squeeze raw dough through the garlic press and push the ends of the resulting strands into the ginger-

bread before baking. It works especially well for fur, hair, and grass, as shown.

Gingerbread

If you want to make a specific addition to your gingerbread house but can't find a suitable candy for the job, consider making it out of gingerbread. Gingerbread can make excellent accessories as well as serve as a sturdy structural base. I have seen it used beautifully to make stairs, fences, door frames, window frames, shutters, and roof tiles. Flat, rounded pieces make ideal stones for pathways and walls. I have used it myself in this book to make the following accessories: a "wooden" drawbridge (Castle, page 80), a stone wall (Country Chapel, page 86), porch posts (Victorian, page 112), and a balcony, door, and shutters (Swiss Chalet, page 106).

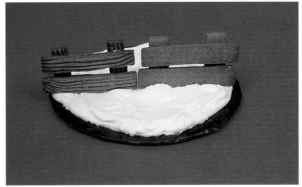

Gold Leaf Roof

Although gold leaf is considered edible in many parts of the world today, the USDA withholds its approval for Americans because, like dragees, it has never been studied (see

page 35). However, it is non-toxic and makes a stunning addition to gingerbread.

To apply gold leaf, first brush the area to be covered with a beaten egg white. Then place the delicate gold leaf onto the egg white and brush flat with a small paintbrush. (Many people like to lift the gold leaves with paintbrushes, too, so their hands don't damage them.) If any part of the gold leaf fails to adhere properly, more beaten egg white may be gently applied on top of it.

Graham Cracker Cottages

Note that the side walls are iced to the side ends of the front wall, not behind it like most other houses. This ensures that the roof fits properly.

 TIP: Six-inch cake circles or Chinet brand paper plates make great bases for graham cracker cottages.

Although they are not really gingerbread houses, graham cracker cottages make great gifts. They also provide an excellent way to share holiday house decorating with a group of people, especially the very young and the very old. (See Taking Your Show on the Road, page 140.) As a general rule of thumb, I would say that most children seven years old and older could assemble the houses themselves before decorating. Children six and under, as well as many elderly people, probably need to have them pre-assembled.

Each graham cracker cottage requires four whole grahams; one box makes six to eight complete houses (generally, name-brand products have thirty-three grahams per box, while off-brands have thirty per box). However, be sure to buy extra to allow for breakage. The houses are very sturdy once assembled, but the crackers sometimes break when being cut.

The key to cutting graham crackers successfully is to use a very sharp, serrated knife in a gentle sawing motion. (Sharpness is more important than serration. If you have to choose between a flat blade and a serrated blade, pick the sharpest one.) Do not press down hard on the knife or the cracker, but slowly work your way down when cutting.

You'll probably want to assemble your cottages at least one day before the big event so that the icing dries thoroughly. Be generous with your royal icing so the houses are sturdy; I like to use a decorating bag with a #8 tip or a hole cut to the approximate size of a #8.

Quick Fact: Gingerbread was so popular during the reign of Queen Elizabeth I that the royal family employed its own gingerbread baker. Queen Elizabeth often gave gingerbread creations to her guests as gifts.

To make the houses:

❶ Use a sharp, serrated knife to cut the front and back walls of the house in the shape shown (square on the bottom half, triangular on the top). I try to make each peak about 3/4" from the top of each graham cracker. While you should try to be consistent, you don't have to have your peaks in precisely the same spot on each cracker. I never know where I am going to make the cuts; I just eyeball the cracker and make my best guess. All of my houses have turned out fine.

❷ After cutting the front and back pieces, break two more graham crackers in half for each house.

❸ Pipe icing from a decorating bag onto the bottom of the house's front wall. Set it on a cake circle or stiff paper plate.

❹ Pipe a line of icing under the side wall and attach it to the sides of the front wall (not behind it as you do on a real gingerbread house; this ensures a properly fitting roof later on).

❺ Pipe a line of icing on both ends of the back wall and under it. Attach it to the inside of the side wall.

❻ Pipe a line of icing on the sides of the front and back walls and under the remaining side wall. Attach the side wall to the house.

❼ Pipe icing around the tops of all of the walls.

❽ Attach the two roof pieces and pipe a line of icing across the roof's peak.

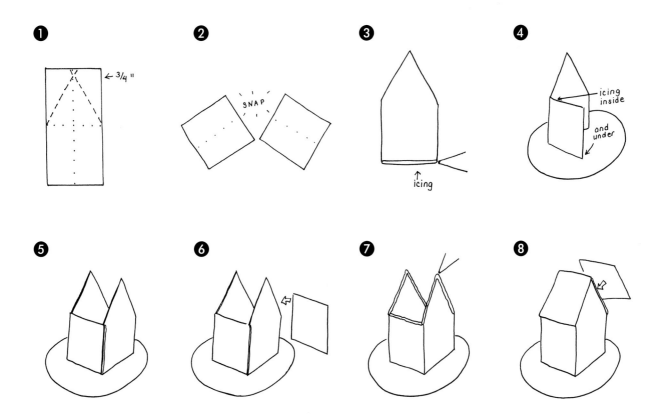

The Grass Tip

Often nicknamed "the grass tip," #233 is a wonderful addition to your decorating tip collection. It is used to make grass, fur, hair, and pine needles. Simply put the tip right up to the place where you want the strands attached, squeeze so that the icing blobs into it, stop squeezing, and pull away. It's easy, but you might want to practice on a plate first.

To make clever pine trees with the grass tip, begin at the bottom of an ice cream sugar cone with green icing and work your way up. When finished, add small pine cones with the #2 or #3 tip. Larger, more detailed pinecones can be added by attaching French burnt peanuts to the pine needles.

Grocery Store Finds

Before and during the holiday season, keep your eyes peeled when you're in the

grocery store for seasonally decorated snacks. Certain items, especially cookies, candy, and cereal, sport special seasonal forms that can instantly enhance your gingerbread creations. Two timesaving baked goods that are frequently available at this time are gingerbread people and tree-shaped cookies and snack cakes.

Ground Coffee

Ground coffee can be used as dirt in the yard of a realistic house.

Gum

Colorful gum looks great where any flat decoration is needed. It can be used for roof tiles, shutters, and doors. It can also be cut and bent to make sleds, benches, mailboxes, and more. The two most colorful brands I've found are Fruit Stripe and Big Red. (See the Pretty Pastel Cottage on page 76.)

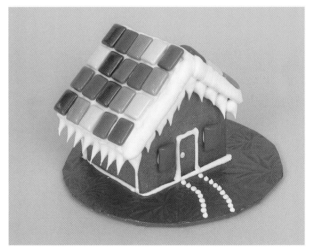

Chiclets and Chiclet-type gum also make great roof tiles, sidewalks, and shutters, and their vivid colors add a lot of pizzazz. Mini-Chiclets work well as gravel or, as in the case of the Birdhouse on page 62, bird food.

Gumpaste

Gumpaste is an edible, pasty, clay-like modeling substance that rolls out extremely thin and dries quite hard. It is often used by cake decorators to make realistic-looking flowers and leaves for cake tops. It is an advanced cake decorating technique that cannot adequately be covered in a paragraph or two. It cannot be overlooked either, though, because many highly skilled decorators have used it in conjunction with gingerbread to create extremely realistic details on their projects, from large sailboats and lighthouses down to tiny little cornices, gargoyles, and other architectural details. It is a fabulous medium to work with, but it also takes a lot of skill. I had the great gumpaste expert, Maureen Stevenson from England, stay at my house for a week several summers ago. As a thank you she gave me private lessons in gumpaste, but I still have trouble with it! However, I'll freely admit that I haven't given the craft of gumpaste the one thing it requires to achieve success—*practice*. You must be willing to devote time and energy to practice gumpaste skills once you have learned them, and you, too, will be able to make the most incredibly realistic, totally edible details for your gingerbread projects.

Gumpaste flowers on this page by Diane Gibbs.

If you would like to learn more about gumpaste, I recommend you take a hands-on class at a local cake decorating store if it's offered. Or, find a book* about gumpaste, buy a can of mix, and practice at home on your own.

Herbs

Fresh herbs make fabulous trees and shrubbery on realistic houses. Full and vibrant when fresh, they still look good when they dry out—a little thinner and duller perhaps, but isn't all greenery in the wintertime? Good choices to consider are rosemary and thyme (this close-up is from the Victorian, page 112). Also, dill draped along a wall or down a banister makes excellent garland.

*Some cake decorating stores have videos on gumpaste, as well as a number of other cake decorating techniques, behind the counter you can rent for a couple of days.

Ice Cream Sugar Cone Trees

These trees are classic to gingerbread houses. The three in the background were formed by using various star tips in a zigzag motion (from left to right: #35, #16, and #32).

The tree in the foreground, with boughs, was made by putting the #32 tip up against the ice cream cone, squeezing, pulling down, and stopping. All of the trees were decorated from the bottom up. Decors were added after every row, because the royal icing quickly becomes too stiff for them to stick.

Icicles

Icicles not only add charm to any gingerbread house they grace, but they can cover up flaws as well. Don't stop to question whether or not they make sense in a particular place, just know that they look good wherever they go.

Icicles can be made with any large round tip from #8 to #12 (or no tip at all), but I usually use the #10. Simply turn your icing

bag upside down underneath the eaves, squeeze a large dab against the gingerbread, stop squeezing, and pull away. Again, it's just squeeze, stop, and pull away. The mistake many beginners make is that they never stop squeezing, which can make for some really long icicles. Sometimes, also, these long ones break away from the gingerbread. If you do make a mistake, just scrape it off and make another—no one will ever know.

Enhancing your icicles with edible glitter adds an extra dimension of sparkle to your work. After every three or four icicles you make, gently blow glitter onto them from a spoon. Not all of the glitter will stick, but that which falls down onto the snow below will look good, too.

Impression Mats

Impression mats are the find of the century. Although a little pricey ($10 to $12 for a set of two), they have so many clever uses that they're well worth the cost. First, they make great stone and brick patterns on the sides of your house walls: just press them into the dough before cutting, lift, trim, and bake. The baked pieces retain the pattern beautifully. Second, they make terrifically easy stone and brick walls. Simply cut your gingerbread into long, thin rectangles after it has been impressed upon, and voila! You have a wonderful wall. Third, the wood pattern makes beautiful doors. I used it to make fondant doors on the A-frame and Candy Cottages (pages 58, 68, 72, and 76 respectively) and to make gingerbread doors on the Victorian and the Castle (pages 112 and 80, respectively). I loved the results and think you will, too.

If impression mats are unavailable, brick, wood, or stone patterns can be carved into the gingerbread with a sharp knife.

Inlay

Inlay is the result of inserting small pieces of light-colored dough into larger pieces of dark-colored dough (or vice versa) and then baking. It is best done with two of the same types of dough, such as light gingerbread dough with dark gingerbread dough, or light sugar cookie dough with dark sugar cookie dough. Mixing dough types can produce air bubbles and other uneven results.

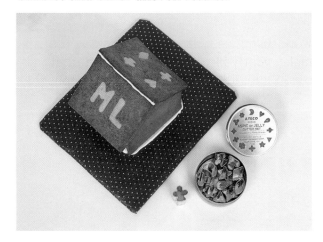

To make an inlaid piece like that shown here, roll out the dough and cut pieces in the desired shape. With small cutters, such as aspic cutters (which were used here), remove these pieces of darker dough. Roll a small piece of the lighter dough and *use the same cutter* to remove a piece of that and insert it into the dark dough. If the piece sticks inside of the cutter, blow gently from the other end. Push the pieces together with your fingers, if necessary, and bake as usual.

Jellybeans

Jellybeans make great walls, especially those that mimic the colors of real stones.

First, squeeze a line of icing where you want the rock wall to go and lay a row of jellybeans. Then, squeeze a line of icing on top of the row and lay another row of jellybeans. Continue until the wall reaches its desired height.

Natural-colored jellybeans also make great stone walkways and rock chimneys in realistic houses. As for fantasy houses, brightly colored jellybeans look good everywhere, but there, too, they make charming walkways and chimneys.

Lace Points

Lace points add delicate elegance to any gingerbread abode—and they are easy to make. Use the lace point pattern provided (see page 47), or make your own. Just remember that the more places the royal icing touches, the stronger the piece will be.

Therefore, this design:

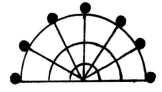

is much sturdier than this:

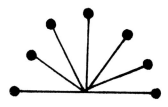

Prepare a board by taping a piece of waxed paper over a pattern, as shown on the next page. With royal icing and a small round tip, such as a #1 or #2, trace the lace point patterns. Let them harden for several hours, then remove them from the waxed paper by sliding a thin sheet of paper under them. Attach them to your house with more royal icing.

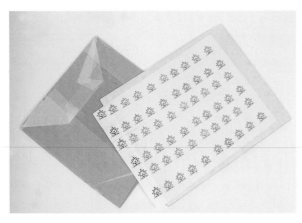

Lace points are delicate and break easily. Make double the amount you think you will need and don't get frustrated if they break while you are attaching them to your house. Once on, though, they will not break unless bumped.

Large Houses

If you are designing your own gingerbread house and it is going to be quite large, consider making some of the pieces the same size as a jelly roll pan (or any pan with short sides). That way, the pan can be used like a mold. Line it with aluminum foil and roll the dough all the way to the pan's sides. If the piece is to be used as a roof, that's all you need to do before baking. If it is a wall, however, you may want to score windows and doors for easy tracing with royal icing after construction. (Windows and doors may also be cut

into the dough, but don't do too many, because the structure will weaken.)

Bake the dough as is in the pan. When the gingerbread cools, it will shrink slightly and be easy to pop right out. If you are worried about the strength of your large structure, add a center wall inside of the building for support.

Lasagna Noodles

The frilled edge of a lasagna noodle makes a great curtain (see the Southwestern Ranch House on page 96).

Lighting the House from Within

Just a few years ago, this section would have been written as a mini-lesson about electricity and how to connect your own small light bulb to an electrical cord. Thank heavens for progress! Now all I need to tell you is to go to your local craft store and ask for a single-bulb craft light. Make a hole in your cake base with a drill or serrated knife and pop in the light.

Your base will either need small legs to lift it above the cord or a channel dug into it, into which the cord is placed. Either method works fine, depending on the type of base you're using, but don't put the base directly on the cord or it will wobble.

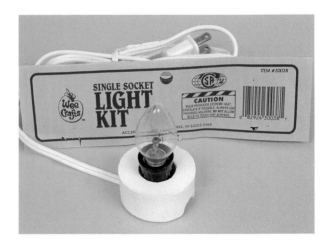

Lace Point Pattern

Log Piles

Log piles can be made with little stacks of Tootsie Rolls, pretzels, cinnamon sticks, or tubular cookies. Some cake stores even sell tiny little sugar axes to lay beside your log pile—or you can make one with a Necco wafer and a thin pretzel stick.

Mailboxes

Mailboxes can be shaped from Tootsie Rolls, caramels, fondant, or marzipan. Add a thin pretzel for a post and top it off with alphabet pasta numbers (see the front lawn of the Suburban Split-level, page 100).

Marshmallow Snowpeople

Three large marshmallows, stacked with royal icing between each one, make cheerful snowpeople. Pretzel arms have been added, along with various decors.

Marzipan

Marzipan is an almond paste that is used in many European countries to form clever, edible, decorative animals and fruits. Many Americans find its flavor an acquired taste, but it is excellent to model with and is readily available. Many cake decorating stores carry marzipan, but a number of well-stocked grocery stores do, too.

Melted Chocolate Trees

Chocolate trees are easily made with the help of a microwave oven. Lay lollipop sticks on baking sheets lined with waxed paper. Melt chocolate chips (or candy melts) inside of an plastic decorating bag, or inside of a resealable zip-type plastic bag. Begin at 30 seconds,

knead bag, and repeat until just melted. Remove from microwave and snip a small hole at the end of the decorating bag or in a corner of the zip-type bag. Squeeze the chocolate onto the sticks in any design and immediately decorate with sprinkles or small candies. Place them in the refrigerator for 10 to 15 minutes to harden.

Mini Molds

These adorable little houses are made from bakeable plastic mini molds. Unlike clear plastic candy molds, which cannot be baked in your oven, mini molds are an opaque white and can withstand temperatures up to 350°. They must, however, be baked on a cookie sheet.

Necco Wafers

Have you forgotten the name of these traditional gingerbread house roof tiles? They're Necco Wafers, and many cake decorating shops carry them specifically during the holiday season, as do some specialty candy stores (like the ones in malls with big candy bins).

Nuts

Anywhere you need a rock, use a nut.

Painting with Paste Colors

Paste color can be painted on gingerbread directly from the jar. It takes many hours to dry thoroughly, but it looks great!

Pasta

The uses of pasta in gingerbread are limited only by your imagination. Here, I used spinach and egg linguine to create the look of a wood cabin. Slightly thicker pieces could be used to make siding on a house. Thin spaghetti could constitute the straw used by one of the three little pigs to create his house. The possibilities are endless!

One interesting phenomenon I found when working with pasta is that the linguine used on the walls stayed flat, while the linguine on the roof warped from the moisture in the royal icing. I had to lay something heavy on top of it to keep it down. Another roof I made with lasagna noodles looked great at first, but quickly warped and rendered itself useless. Any physics teachers reading this book are more than welcome to e-mail me an explanation of this unusual occurrence.

Pecans

This plucky roof was made with pecans.

Piping Gel Ponds

Piping gel ponds give the look of cool, fresh water and are easy to make: simply add blue paste color to piping gel (shown here) to make "water." However, note that the board underneath the pond needs to be iced with white royal icing before the gel is spread so that the blue water shines.

Piping gel ponds will dry and crack after a day or two, but adding a little glycerin to the gel will help them keep for a week or longer. To achieve the look of a frozen pond, see Crushed Candy Ponds on page 33.

Popcorn Balls

Popcorn balls can be used to make clever bushes and trees. Tint them green, put them on a stick, and attach red hot candies to make a charming little cherry tree. I have found that those made from scratch work the best.

Powdered Sugar

To replicate a light snowfall, sprinkle your project with powdered sugar when finished.

Pre-baked Pieces

A section on pre-baked pieces in a craft book? Isn't that cheating? Only if you are trying to enter your creation in a contest. If you are too busy to bake the gingerbread yourself, or if you are simply uninterested in that aspect of the project, there is nothing wrong with buying pre-baked pieces. It will save time and decrease stress, for most of the joy is in the decorating anyhow.

Many cake decorating stores carry pre-baked gingerbread pieces during the holiday season, and many other types of craft stores sell whole kits which can still be supplemented with additional candy if you wish.

Pretzels

Pretzels are a gingerbread baker's best friend. Coming in a variety of shapes and sizes, they can be used to make a number of different decorations, including log cabin walls, stick and thatched Hawaiian-like roofs, log piles, fences, and posts for mailboxes, swingsets, and other common yard items. Anywhere you need a food product to look like wood or sticks, you can probably find a specific pretzel to get the job done.

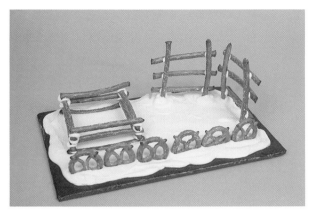

When making a stick fence like the one on the left side of the photo, assemble the individual sections first and let dry before placing them upright in the yard. When making a stick fence like the one on the right side of the photo, lay all of the bottom bars first, each about a half pretzel length away from the one next to it. Then put a dot of icing on the end of each pretzel and lay a second row on top of them. Proceed to a third and even fourth row in the same manner, if desired. The twisted pretzel fence in the foreground of the photograph is by far the easiest to make—just put them upside down in royal icing—but it is still adorable to look at.

Rice Krispy Treats

Rice Krispy Treats, tinted green, make an excellent shrub border for the perimeter of a gingerbread board. They can also be formed into balls and put on sticks to make engaging trees. Conveniently, the ready-made Rice Krispy Treats available in the cereal aisle of most grocery stores work well if you choose not to make your own from scratch. If you wish to make them green, however, you must spray them with a food airbrush or Creative Color Food Spray.

Rice Paper Windows

Whenever I give a demonstration at my children's schools, I like to call them up to take a big bite of rice paper in front of their friends. It tastes pretty good and the audience loves it! That's because rice paper, also called wafer paper, is completely edible. You can draw and paint on it just like regular paper,

but instead of using markers and paints, you use food-coloring pens and paste colors (liquid food colors are too watery). The windows shown here were made with both techniques.

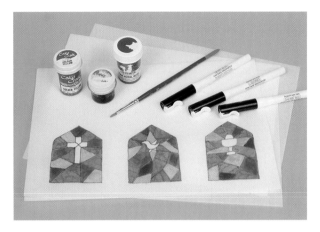

If you use rice paper or any other exotic, but edible, food item in a gingerbread contest, it is perfectly acceptable to leave the judge a note explaining what you've used. That way, no points will be deducted during judging for non-food items.

Rock Candy Hedges

I keep expecting the girls at the mall to stop me from picking out only the green rock candy from the candy bins, but they never do. I find they make adorable hedges, as seen on the A-frame, page 58.

Run Sugar (see Color Flow, page 32)

Sandpaper

New, clean sandpaper works great to smooth down bumpy or misshapen ginger-

bread. It is especially useful with rounded surfaces, such as the gingerbread bowl or the World (see page 118). Coarse sandpaper is quicker and more effective than fine, but the abrasion from either will lighten the look of the dough.

Scalloped Borders

The Garrett Frill Cutter at the top of the picture is a common gumpaste tool that makes excellent scalloped borders in gingerbread, fondant, and gumpaste. The scalloped edge rulers at the bottom achieve the same look when used in conjunction with a sharp knife. They are available in the memory book section of most large craft stores.

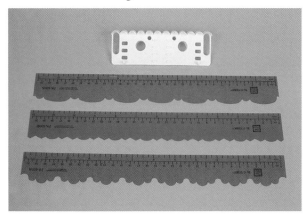

Scoring Windows and Doors

Not every gingerbread house needs to have its windows cut out and decorated with fancy lace curtains or colorful stained glass. Solid gingerbread windows enhanced with royal icing and candy look great, too. One method of achieving perfectly even, well-placed windows and doors is to score the outlines for them into the gingerbread before baking. Use a ruler or straight pattern piece as

Quick Fact: Gingerbread cake is said to be the oldest cake in the world, invented by a Greek from Rhodes about 2000BC. It soon became famous throughout the Mediterranean area.

a guide. The lines will not disappear during the baking process, so when the gingerbread has cooled you can simply trace them with royal icing. Your lines will be straight and uniform.

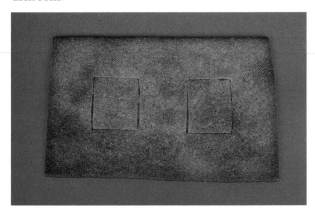

Sheet Gelatin

Sheet gelatin makes beautiful windows for gingerbread houses and it is edible. It can be found in some gourmet food shops and cake decorating stores, and some mail order companies sell it bulk, but Beryl's is the only mail order company I know of that sells it in the

small quantities needed for most gingerbread work (see Resources, pages 183 and 184).

As beautiful as it looks in windows, sheet gelatin can curve and break away from walls after a month or so. Therefore, you probably want to ice it down flat with long scraps (bars) of gingerbread to prevent this from happening.

For spectacular stained glass windows, paint paste colors directly onto sheet gelatin (liquid food colors are too watery). Although the surface won't dry for weeks, the windows can be attached inside your house as soon as they're made. Again, ice them down with strips of gingerbread so that they don't bow and break later.

Shredded Wheat

Large shredded wheat, when broken into long strands, makes an excellent thatched roof. Shredded Mini-wheats left whole are excellent, too, and they even have a sugar-coated side that looks like snow.

Spearmint Leaf Trees

To make evergreens from spearmint leaf candy, cut each piece in half lengthwise. Start at the bottom of an ice cream sugar cone and ice each leaf to it with green royal icing, pointy side down. It takes approximately fourteen candies per tree. The result is an adorable, but surprisingly heavy, little tree (see the A-frame, page 58).

Standing Things Upright

There are a number of things you can do to help a decoration, such as a mailbox or a lamppost, stand upright:
• Insert it into a big pile of royal icing.
• Stick it in a gumdrop, then surround the gumdrop with icing so it doesn't show.
• Stand it in melted chocolate, which hardens quickly.
• Dig or drill a hole into the baseboard, insert the item, and surround it with icing.

Sunflower Seeds

Sunflower seeds can be used to make wonderful fieldstone chimneys.

Tea Leaves

The great cake decorator, author, and instructor from South Africa, Eleanor Reindeer, shared this idea with me: for a realistic mulch around the base of your trees, use tea leaves. They also make great leaf piles when placed with a rake near an autumn abode.

Three-dimensional Cookie Trees

Three-dimensional cookie trees give depth to your work. With a cookie cutter, cut several trees, but before baking, cut some of them in half lengthwise. After baking, ice the half trees to the sides of the whole trees, and you will have freestanding foliage. Of course, this method also works well with cacti and shrubbery.

Tree Formers

A tree former is a handy item that helps you hold an ice cream sugar cone when you're making a pine tree. Put a little dab of icing on the former so that the cone doesn't slide around when you're decorating it. When finished, stick the entire ensemble into Styrofoam or a glass bottle until the tree is dry. Tree formers are available at many cake decorating stores or mail order companies (see Resources, pages 183-186).

Quick Fact: The art of carving detailed molds to create ornate gingerbread cookies in the shapes of animals, angels, windmills, wreaths, letters, and kings and queens was developed in Nuremberg, Germany, the "Gingerbread Capital of the World."

Tremendous Trees

To make big trees, stack two waffle cones together. (One alone will not have a flat enough base, but two staggered is just right.) Large waffle cones are available at most grocery stores, and super-size waffle cones can be found at ice cream shops.

Triscuits

Triscuit snack crackers were used to make this dapper roof.

Wafer Paper (see Rice Paper Windows, page 51)

Wreaths

Use tip #235 (shown on page 22, far right) to make perfect little Christmas wreaths on waxed paper. Bows and berries can be added with any small round tip, such as a #1 or #2.

Large wreaths are made by making a circle of stars with a small star tip, as shown in the photo. Slip a circle pattern under your waxed paper to ensure roundness. Good tips with which to make large wreaths are #20 and #35. Again, add berries and bows with a small round tip.

Chapter 4

Projects and Patterns: A Baker's Dozen

Whereas Chapter 3 was similar to a do-it-yourself super-store, this chapter is like a specialty kitchen and bath design store. Just as you can walk into one of those shops and see a beautiful room ready for duplication in your own home, you can look through this chapter and find gingerbread projects to duplicate in your own kitchen. The finished project is here for viewing, and all patterns and instructions for the project are provided.

This chapter contains a baker's dozen of projects and patterns, all of which can be made by every home baker. Most of them are quite easy to do, but even the slightly more difficult ones aren't beyond the average craftsperson's ability, provided they have a little experience or a lot of motivation. Indeed, most of the following structures are based on the simple pattern of four walls and a roof. The two exceptions to this are the A-frame and the World. The A-frame is the simplest of all, consisting of two walls and a roof, and the World is a round gingerbread globe that is made by using a ball pan. Creating the World is not particularly difficult, but it is labor-intensive. You might want to wait until you have had some experience with gingerbread before tackling it, because decorating gingerbread, like most other craft projects, gets much easier and quicker over time. Whatever you choose, I hope you have as much fun re-creating these homes as I had designing them. Enjoy!

Page 58

Note: Some of the patterns in this chapter need to be enlarged; these patterns are marked as such.

Page 62

Page 68

Page 72

Page 76

Page 80

Page 86

Page 92

Page 96

Page 100

Page 106

Page 112

Page 118

A-frame

Difficulty Level: Super Easy

This sturdy A-frame, consisting of only four pieces of dough, is the easiest of the gingerbread houses to make. I think it's as attractive as the real thing, too. Evidently my cousin Killian agreed; she carried the entire project, only partially boxed because it was so big, on her lap on a bus ride from Baltimore to New York City. Although it was jostled throughout the four-hour ride, not a piece came loose, hence the description of sturdy. Her new husband Jeff thought that she was crazy, my own husband marveled at her determination, and I was simply flattered by the effort she exerted to take this house home.

Materials and Supplies

Copy of the pattern
Board (16" circle or larger)
Foil, any color, if desired
1 batch basic gingerbread recipe
1 batch royal icing
Powdered sugar
2" ball of fondant
1 bag spearmint leaf candy
2 ice cream sugar cones
10 small red flowers*
11 red poinsettias*

6 pieces of Dentine gum
3 candle sets*
1 silver dragee
1 bag red Starlight mints
1 bag green Starlight mints
4 Starburst candies
1 green sugar stick
White edible glitter
Approx. 24 Christmas "lights"*
1 lb. green rock candy
1/2 cup Red Hots

1 decorating bag with coupler
Tips: #3 and #10
Paste colors: green and yellow
"Wood" pattern impression mat, rolling pin, small sharp knife, cans, spreading knife, spoon, non-toxic pencil, ruler

*These items were purchased ready-made at a cake-decorating store.

TIP: Remember to rest the tip of the decorating bag against a damp paper towel between uses.

Day One: Baking the A-frame and Making the Door

❶ Cut out the pattern.

❷ Make the house: Mix the gingerbread dough. Roll, cut, and bake the A-frame pieces according to the directions on pages 16-18. With only four pieces to the A-frame, this should be quick and easy.

❸ Make the door: Work a small amount of yellow paste color into the fondant. Roll flat. Dust the impression mat with powdered sugar and press it into the fondant. Lift it up and cut out the door.

❹ Let all pieces harden overnight.

Day Two: Assembling and Decorating

❶ If desired, cover the board with foil.

❷ Load the decorating bag with the coupler, #10 tip, and white icing.

❸ Ice the back wall toward the back of the board. Reinforce the seam both in front of and behind the wall. Hold upright with cans.

❹ Ice the front wall to the board, about 5" from the back wall. Hold upright with cans.

❺ Squeeze a line of icing up the front wall and the back wall on the left side. Also, run a line of icing across the board, between the walls on the left side.

❻ Lay the roof on the left side of the house. Reinforce all seams, both inside and out. Run a line of icing all of the way around the right side of the building. Lay the right roof down. Reinforce all of its outside seams.

❼ Let the structure dry for approximately 20 minutes. During this time you can unwrap candies, change the tip on the decorating bag to the #3, and tint 1 cup of icing green.

❽ Make the trees: Turn the spearmint leaf candies on their sides and cut them in half lengthwise with the small sharp knife. (Note: Each tree needs approx. fourteen candies.)

❾ With green icing and the spreading knife, ice the spearmint leaves to the ice cream sugar cones, pointy side down. Start at the bottom of each cone and work your way up. After the leaves have been attached to the trees, decorate with the small red flowers and top each with a poinsettia.

❿ Decorate the house: Using the pencil and ruler, draw diagonal lines on the roof where you want white icing to go. Turn the ruler around and draw diagonal lines the other way, forming diamonds.

⓫ With white icing and the #3 tip, trace the pencil marks. Also trace the outline of the three windows on the front of the house.

Note: See photo of the completed A-frame for suggested decoration placement.

⓬ Still with the white icing and #3 tip, affix the following to the front of the house:
- 6 pieces of gum for shutters
- 3 candle sets in the windows
- 6 poinsettias on the shutters
- 2 additional poinsettias on the front wall of the house
- Fondant front door
- Silver dragee as the doorknob
- Red and green Starlight mints to the roof, in the center of each diamond (watch for sliding)

⓭ With the white icing and #3 tip, make bows on the Starbursts to create presents for the front yard.

⓮ Change to the #10 tip and use white icing to attach the sugar stick to the roof's peak and a poinsettia to the peak's front.

⓯ Sprinkle edible glitter on the roof.

⓰ Still with the #10 tip, make icicles under the eaves. After every third or fourth icicle, gently blow on edible glitter from a spoon.

⓱ Squeeze a dab of icing on the back of each colored light and add to the front of the house.

⓲ Spread white icing on the yard with the knife, one section at a time. Sprinkle with edible glitter as you go. Also, lay the Red Hots for the sidewalk, rock candy for the shrubbery in front of the house and around the perimeter of the board, sugar cone trees, and Starburst presents.

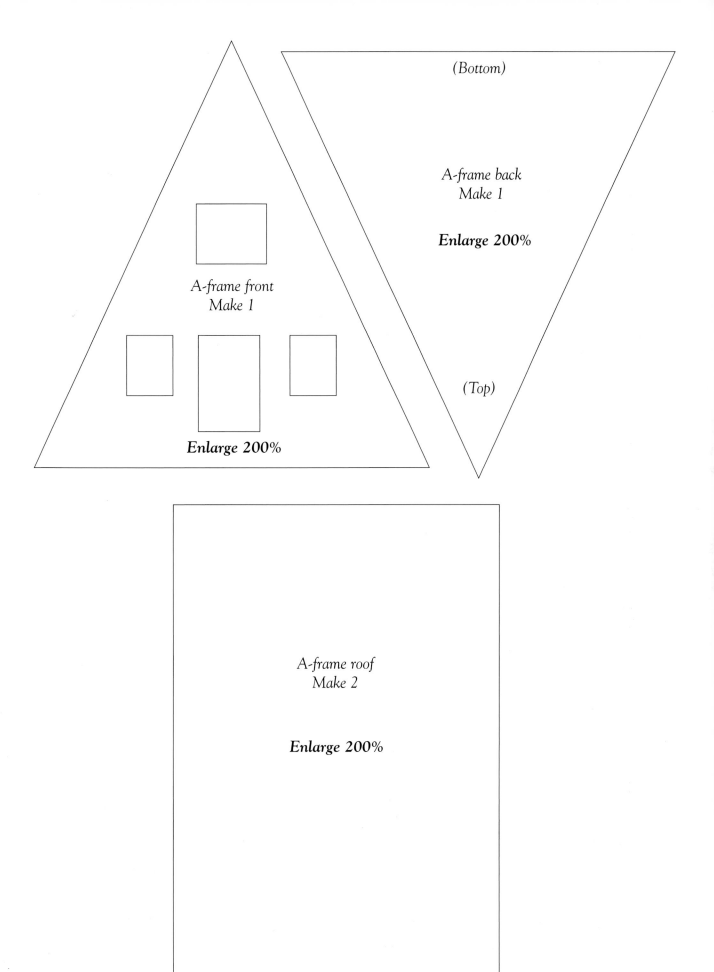

(Bottom)

A-frame back
Make 1

Enlarge 200%

A-frame front
Make 1

Enlarge 200%

(Top)

A-frame roof
Make 2

Enlarge 200%

Birdhouse

Tweet! Tweet! Tweet! What bird wouldn't chirp with happiness to be living in this neat and sweet floral retreat? It's a perfect centerpiece at any time of year and it's super easy to make. You can use it as a spectacular, semi-permanent way to showcase your flower-making talents, if you like to make your own flowers. Or, if you buy them ready-made from a cake decorating store, you can complete the entire project in a single afternoon. Either way, this project will have everyone twittering with admiration.

Materials and Supplies

Copy of the pattern
Board (12" circle or larger)
Foil, any color, if desired
1 batch basic gingerbread recipe
1 batch royal icing
Craft birds: 1 large and 2 small

1 pretzel stick
Flowers: Approx. 4 large, 35 medium, and 15 small
Mini-Chiclets*
3 decorating bags, 2 with couplers
Tips: #10, #21, #3, #67, #352, and #113

Paste colors: brown and leaf green

*These are often available at the check-out lines in grocery stores

Day One: Baking the Birdhouse

❶ Cut out the pattern.

❷ Make the house: Mix the gingerbread dough. Cut, roll, and bake the Birdhouse pieces according to the directions on pages 16-18.

❸ If you are making your own flowers, make them as well.

 TIP: To learn how to make your own flowers, take a decorating class at a local cake store or refer to books listed in the Related Books section on pages 187 and 188.

TIP: Remember to rest the tips of the decorating bags against damp paper towels between uses.

Day Two: Assembling and Decorating

❶ If desired, cover the board with foil.

❷ Tint half of the icing brown, the other half leaf green.

❸ Load one of the decorating bags with a coupler, brown icing, and the #10 tip. Assemble the Birdhouse according to the directions on pages 24 and 25. Although the lower walls slant outward, this should not prove to be unduly problematic as long as you have a good stiff batch of icing. Don't reinforce the seams on the outside of the Birdhouse, though, until you change to a decorative tip (see the next step).

❹ Change to the #21 tip and make a series of evenly sized stars to reinforce the outer seams.

❺ Still with the brown icing, perch the two small birds inside of the large hole and the pretzel in the small hole.

❻ Put a coupler in another decorating bag and load with green icing, but do not attach a tip.

Note: See photo of the completed Birdhouse for suggested flower placement.

❼ Make a big, long, green blob on the top right side of the roof, under the spot where the bulk of the flowers are going to be placed.

❽ Arrange the flowers on the blob, tilting slightly toward the front, the largest ones first, leaving gaps between them for leaves. (Reserve some small and medium flowers for Step 11.)

❾ Put the #113 tip into the end of the last decorating bag and fill with green icing. Use it to make large leaves in the areas where there are large gaps between the flowers.

❿ Attach the #67 tip to the decorating bag with green icing and coupler (from Step 5-7). Make smaller leaves between the large leaves and flowers.

⓫ Change to the #3 tip and make a few vines climbing up the front and sides of the Birdhouse.

⓬ Place the remaining small and medium flowers on the vines with little dabs of icing.

⓭ Change to the #352 tip and fill in the area around the flowers with leaves.

⓮ Attach the large bird to the base with brown icing.

⓯ Scatter Mini-Chiclet "seeds" to look like bird food in front of the house.

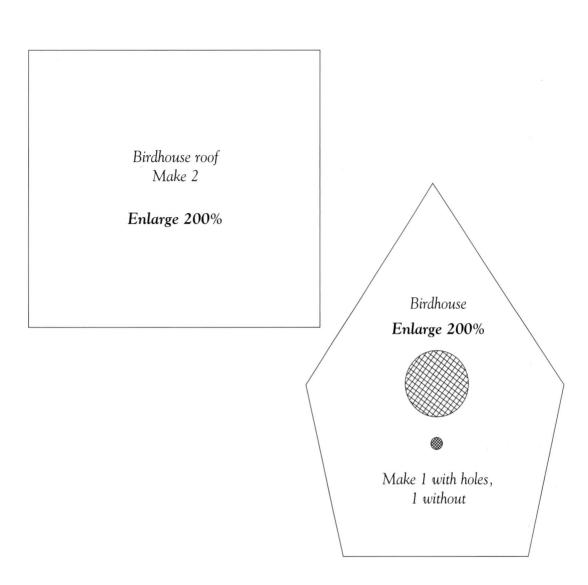

Birdhouse roof
Make 2

Enlarge 200%

Birdhouse
Enlarge 200%

Make 1 with holes,
1 without

Birdhouse wall
Make 2

Candy Cottage Pattern

The next three gingerbread houses are variations on a theme. The Fondant Roof Cottage, Hansel and Gretel House, and Pretty Pastel Cottage all use the simple pattern below. I call it the Candy Cottage Pattern.

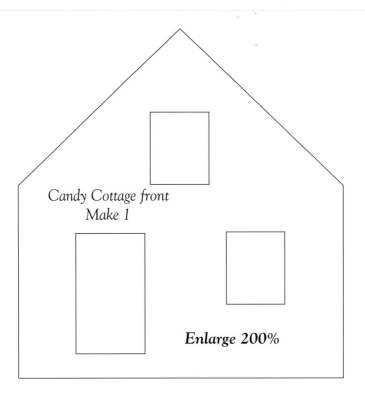

Candy Cottage front
Make 1

Enlarge 200%

Candy Cottage roof
Make 2

(Top)

(Bottom)

Enlarge 200%

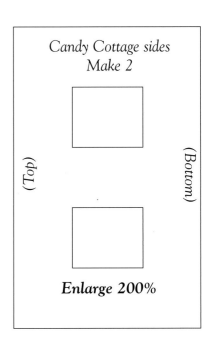

Candy Cottage sides
Make 2

(Top)

(Bottom)

Enlarge 200%

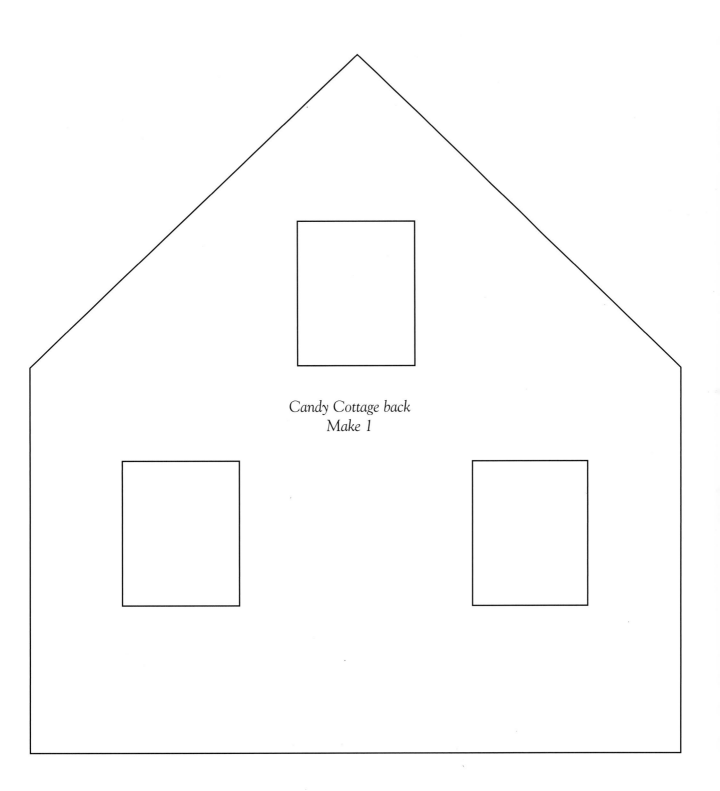

Candy Cottage back
Make 1

Fondant Roof Cottage or Santa in the Off-season

Difficulty Level: Easy

The Christmas decorations are packed away, the elves are on vacation, and Mrs. Claus is taking a nap. Santa, however, stands outside of his snowy abode, warmly welcoming guests during his off-season. There's still the air of Christmas—this is the North Pole after all—but it's the glittery fondant rooftop and the shiny gold shutters that truly draw the visitor's eye. Come in, sit down, warm up, and tell Santa how your year is progressing; he is always happy to hear.

Materials and Supplies

Copy of the pattern
Board (16" circle or larger)
Foil, any color, if desired
Board for rolling the fondant
1 batch basic gingerbread recipe
1 batch royal icing
1 lb. fondant
Powdered sugar
1/2 foot lace trim
Cookies*

Gold luster dust
Pearl dust
11 red raspberry gummis
13 dragees
1 red Starlight mint
27 candy canes
Edible glitter
1/2 lb. green rock candy
Malted milk crunch
1 Santa figurine
1 decorating bag with coupler

Tips: #3 and #10
"Wood" pattern impression mat, sharp serrated knife, spreading knife, small dry paint brush, spoon, rolling pin, paper towel

*Healthy Valley Original Rice Bran Crackers—from a gourmet shop—are shown here.

Day One: Baking the Cottage and Making the Door

❶ Cut out the pattern.

❷ Make the house: Mix the gingerbread dough. Roll, cut, and bake the Cottage pieces according to the directions on pages 16-18.

❸ Make the door: Sprinkle the fondant board with powdered sugar and roll a 2" ball of fondant flat. Dust the impression mat with powdered sugar and press into the fondant. Remove mat and trim fondant.

❹ Let all pieces harden overnight.

 TIP: Remember to rest the tip of the decorating bag against a damp paper towel between uses.

Day Two: Assembling and Decorating

❶ If desired, cover the board with foil.

❷ Cut the lace trim down to 1-1/2" pieces and affix to the insides of the window frames with white icing.

❸ Assemble the Cottage according to the directions on pages 24 and 25.

 TIP: Having an assistant hold the board up above the roof for you makes it much easier for you to slide the fondant onto the roof accurately.

❹ Make the fondant roof: Sprinkle the fondant board with powdered sugar. Roll the fondant out flat. Important: To prevent sticking, pick up the fondant and turn it a half turn between every one or two rolls of the rolling pin. Sprinkle with powdered sugar as needed. When the fondant slab has reached the desired size (slightly larger than the roof) quickly prepare the roof by spreading it with a thin layer of icing.

❺ Lift the board with the fondant on it up to the roof and gently slide the fondant onto the roof.

❻ Smooth the fondant, trim it, and fold the edges under the edge of the roof.

❼ With the sharp serrated knife, trim the cookies down to shutter size.

 TIP: To trim crispy cookies, use a sharp serrated knife and a gentle, sawing motion.

❽ Use the paintbrush to dust the shutters and the welcome mat cookies with gold luster dust. Clean the brush by rubbing the bristles on a paper towel. Do not use water.

❾ Dust the fondant front door with pearl dust.

Note: See photo of the completed Cottage for suggested decoration placement.

❿ Load the decorating bag with the coupler, #3 tip, and white icing and attach the following to the house:

- 11 red raspberry gummis to the rooftop
- 11 gold dragees to the red raspberry gummis
- 1 red Starlight mint to the front of the roof's peak
- Cookie shutters to the window frames
- Fondant front door
- 1 dragee as a doorknob

⓫ Still with white icing and #3 tip, make decorative designs above the windows and door.

⓬ With the sharp, serrated knife, trim the candy canes down to where they form a "U."

 TIP: The icing must be wet for the edible glitter to adhere.

⓭ Spread icing in a thick layer around the front yard, one section at a time. Sprinkle with edible glitter as you go.

⓮ Place green rock candy as hedges around the house.

⓯ Press the malted milk candy into the icing to make a sidewalk in front of the house.

⓰ Insert the candy cane "U"s into the snow around the yard's perimeter.

⓱ Place the Santa figurine in the front yard.

⓲ With white icing and the #10 tip, affix the welcome mat outside of the front door.

⓳ Pipe a line of icing atop the hedges. Sprinkle with edible glitter.

⓴ Form icicles underneath the eaves. After every third or fourth icicle, apply edible glitter by gently blowing it onto the icicles from a spoon.

㉑ Dip the paintbrush in water and lightly wet the fondant roof. Generously sprinkle with edible glitter.

Hansel and Gretel House

Difficulty Level: Easy

The original story of Hansel and Gretel, like many of Grimms' fairy tales, is quite gruesome.

During a period of great famine in Germany, a cruel stepmother decided that she and her husband could no longer support his two children. He reluctantly agreed to abandon them in the woods. Hansel and Gretel overheard their evil plan, and when they were led deep into the woods, Hansel dropped a series of white pebbles which enabled them to find their way home later that night.

Their father was secretly delighted at their return, but their stepmother was enraged. The following day the children were again led away. This time Hansel was unable to leave a trail of pebbles, so he dropped breadcrumbs instead. When the children tried to find their way home later that night, they found that the birds had eaten all of the breadcrumbs and they were hopelessly lost.

After wandering around the forest for many days, Hansel and Gretel stumbled across a beautiful gingerbread cottage covered with cookie and candy confections. They hungrily began to eat the cottage. When an old woman came out and offered them beds of downy white on which to sleep, they eagerly accepted.

Unfortunately, the children soon discovered that the old woman was actually a wicked witch, and she locked Hansel up in a chicken coop. Her plan was to fatten him up before she cooked and ate him. Gretel was forced to cook for him and serve them both.

When the time came for Hansel to be eaten, the witch commanded Gretel to light the fire in the oven. Gretel pretended that she didn't know how. When the wicked witch bent over to show her, Gretel pushed her into the oven and the witch perished.

Gretel released her brother from the chicken coop, they filled their pockets with pearls they found inside of the gingerbread house, and they managed to find their way home. A joyous reunion took place between father and offspring, for in their absence their evil stepmother had died. They all lived happily ever after.

(Most people who make this project are going to use cookies and candies they like best, but I am supplying my list and instructions in case someone wants to know exactly what was used here and how it was done.)

Copy of the pattern
Board (16" circle or larger)
Foil, any color, if desired
1 batch basic gingerbread recipe
2 batches royal icing
2" ball of fondant
Alphabet pasta*
Powdered sugar
12 Pepperidge Farm Chessman cookies
20 gumdrops
10 Skittles
10 Sweetarts
12 large silver dragees
Approx. 40 small flowers

1 sugar stick
2 Junior Mints
12 Air Crisp Pretzels
20 spearmint leaf candies
1/8 cup red decors
6 rock candy lollipops
6 root beer barrels
2 decorating bags, 1 with coupler
Tips: #10, #233, #349, and others if desired to decorate gingerbread people
Paste color: green, as well as other desired colors to decorate gingerbread people
Small paintbrush, spreading

knife, large gingerbread woman cookie cutter, small gingerbread boy cookie cutter, small gingerbread girl cookie cutter

*See Day One, Step 5, and Day Two, Step 10, for needed letters.

Day One: Baking the House and Making the Accessories

❶ Cut out the pattern.

❷ Make the house: Mix the gingerbread. Roll, cut, and bake the House according to the directions on pages 16-18.

❸ Cut and bake the gingerbread people: one woman, one boy, and one girl.

❹ Cut and bake a 1-1/2" x 3" gingerbread cookie for the welcome mat.

❺ Decorate the wicked witch, Hansel, and Gretel as desired.

❻ Decorate the welcome mat (see Color Flow page 32): Thin 2 tablespoons of icing with 1/2-teaspoon water. Tint with the desired paste color and brush onto the rectangular cookie with the small paintbrush. Add alphabet pasta letters to read "ENTER AT YOUR OWN RISK."

❼ Sprinkle your work surface with powdered sugar. Roll out the fondant and cut six 2 x 2-1/2" crossbars for the windows.

❽ Let all pieces dry overnight.

TIP: *Remember to rest the tips of the decorating bags against damp paper towels between uses.*

Day Two: Assembling and Decorating

❶ If desired, cover the board with foil.

❷ Load one of the decorating bags with white icing and the #10 tip.

❸ Attach the fondant crossbars to the insides of the window frames with dabs of icing.

❹ Assemble the gingerbread house according to the directions on pages 24 and 25. Place it toward the back of the board so there is room in front for Hansel, Gretel, and the wicked witch.

Note: See photo of the completed House for suggested decoration placement.

5 Spread a thin layer of white icing on the roof and attach the following sweets:
- 12 Chessman cookies
- 14 of the gumdrops
- 10 Skittles
- 10 Sweetarts
- 12 silver dragees
- Assorted flowers, reserving some for Steps 6 and 13

6 Using the decorating bag and #10 tip, ice the sugar stick to the peak of the roof and cap the ends with Junior Mints.

7 Attach the Air Crisp Pretzels as shutters to the sides of the windows. Affix one small flower to each shutter.

8 Still with white icing and the #10 tip, form icicles under the eaves.

9 Tint all of the remaining icing green.

10 Load the remaining decorating bag with the coupler, green icing, and #349 tip. Add leaves to the flowers on the shutters; also attach flowers to the window sills.

11 Affix the word "WELCOME" over the front door using alphabet pasta.

12 With the knife, spread a thin layer of green icing around the house. Add spearmint leaf candies as bushes around the house and sprinkle red decors in front of the house to make a pathway.

13 Insert the ends of the rock candy lollipops into the remaining gumdrops to make trees.

14 Change the bag with green icing to the #233 tip and landscape the yard. Add the people, remaining flowers, root beer barrels, and rock candy trees in small mounds of icing as you go.

15 Affix the welcome mat near the front door.

Pretty Pastel Cottage

Difficulty Level: Easy

This cottage is the first house I made for the book. It is also the first house I gave away, to our friend Carol Kershner as she battled cancer. I am happy to report that the cancer is now completely eradicated, but gingerbread house lives on. Sometimes things do work out the way they are supposed to.

Materials and Supplies

Copy of the pattern
Board (16" circle or larger)
Foil, any color, if desired
1 batch basic gingerbread recipe
1 batch royal icing
1 lb. fondant
Powdered sugar
1 pack Fruit Stripe gum
1 gumdrop
1 tiny piece of Fruit Roll-Up

1/2 lb. pastel mint chips
1 pastel-colored sugar stick
2 candy necklaces (cut apart)
1/8 cup metallic dragees
Approx. 13 flowers
3 yellow candy melts
1 bag spearmint leaf candies
4 Starburst candies
8 Necco Wafers
1 cup thin pretzel sticks

4 decorating bags, 1 with coupler
Tips #2, #3, #10, #21, and #349
Paste colors: yellow, green, and blue
"Wood" pattern impression mat, rolling pin, serrated rolling pin, small sharp knife, spreading knife, ruler, non-toxic pencil (optional)

Day One: Baking the House and Making the Accessories

1 Cut out the pattern.

2 Make the house: Mix the gingerbread. Roll, cut, and bake the Candy Cottage according to the directions on pages 16-18.

3 Make the window crossbars: Lightly dust your work space with powdered sugar and roll out a large pinch of fondant. Cut six crossbars for the windows, approximately 2" x 2-1/2".

4 Make the doors and shutters: Tint the remaining fondant blue. Lightly dust your work space with powdered sugar and roll the fondant flat. Dust the impression mat with powdered sugar and press into the fondant. Lift and cut out the front door. Roll the serrated rolling pin over the rest of the fondant. Cut twelve 1/2" x 1-1/2" shutters.

5 Cut three or more decorative hearts from the remaining blue fondant.

6 Load one of the decorating bags with white icing and the #2 tip. Referring to the completed pieces in the photo, cut, fold, and ice together the Fruit Stripe gum to make the garden bench and sled.

7 Again referring to the photo, bend a piece of Fruit Stripe gum into the shape of a mailbox. With the small sharp knife, cut two small, arched pieces for the front and the back of the mailbox. Cut a flag from the piece of Fruit Roll-Up. Assemble with white icing.

8 Let all pieces dry overnight.

TIP: Remember to rest the tips of the decorating bags against damp paper towels between uses.

Day Two: Assembling and Decorating

1 If desired, cover the board with foil.

2 Load one of the decorating bags with the coupler, white icing, and #10 tip.

3 Attach the crossbars to the insides of the window frames with dabs of icing.

4 Assemble the Candy Cottage according to the directions on pages 24 and 25.

5 Mark off where the scallops are to go on the roof: Use the ruler to measure 1" increments along the roof, then mark the spots with a non-toxic pencil or small dots of icing.

Note: See photo of the completed Cottage for suggested decoration placement.

6 Change to the #3 tip and make scallops with white icing. Snip the peaks off of the mint chips and affix to ends of each scallop.

7 Still with the #3 tip, affix the following to the house:

- Sugar stick to the roof's peak
- Candy necklace pieces, removed from their string, to the front of the roof and the side wall seams
- Blue fondant front door
- 1 dragee as a doorknob
- Flowers on the window sills
- 3 yellow candy melts
- Blue fondant hearts on top of the candy melts
- Dragees on top of the hearts

8 Still with the white icing and #3 tip, add icicles under the eaves.

9 Switch to the #21 tip and make a shell border around the sugar stick. Also form a star on each end of the sugar stick.

10 Tint 1/4 cup of the icing light green. Load one of the decorating bags with green icing and the #349 tip. Form leaves on the flower bunches on the windowsills.

11 Using the spreading knife, begin icing the front yard, one section at a time, with white icing. Add spearmint leaf candies as bushes to the front and sides of the house as you ice. Also stack the Starbursts in front of the front door to make steps and lay down the Necco Wafers to form a sidewalk. Arrange the Fruit Stripe gum lawn decorations made the day before around the lawn.

12 Make the fence: Lay a row of pretzels around the perimeter of the yard, each about a half a pretzel length from the one before it. Put a dab of icing on the end of each pretzel and lay another row of pretzels on top. Ice those ends and lay a third row.

13 Switch the decorating bag with white icing back to the #3 tip and decorate the fence with swags of icing. Add a dragee at the top of each swag.

14 Tint 1/4 cup of the icing yellow.

15 Load the remaining decorating bag with yellow icing and the #2 tip and make a bow on top of each spearmint leaf bush in the front yard.

Castle

Difficulty Level: Moderately Easy

Droofus the Dragon faithfully guards the drawbridge of this cute castle. The structure itself consists of four basic walls and an inlaid roof, but it's the attention to detail that completes the scene. Ice cream sugar cone turrets, sheet gelatin windows, stone walls, a wooden drawbridge, and a rock border lend it the authentic air it needs to become a most regal abode.

This castle can also be made with the drawbridge up* and then filled with candy for an extra-special treat to delight the children on the day the walls must come down. Keep the sheet gelatin in the window so the kids can get a glimpse of the goodies within, and remember to do the following: 1) Use a lot of icing to reinforce the seams both inside and out; 2) Let it dry completely before adding the roof; and 3) Don't overstuff it. Your candy-filled castle is a guaranteed winner!

Materials and Supplies

Copy of the pattern
Board (16" circle or larger)
Foil, any color, if desired
2 batches basic gingerbread recipe
1 batch royal icing
Powdered sugar
1/4 lb. fondant
5 lollipop sticks
2 sheets of sheet gelatin*
1 cup piping gel
1 lb. jellybeans

2 cups coconut
1/3 cup Grape Nuts cereal
2 caramels
5 ice cream cones
9 decorative flowers
1 dragon figurine
2 decorating bags, 1 with coupler
Tips: #10, #3, and #28
Paste colors: red, yellow, brown, blue, and green

"Stone" pattern impression mat, "wood" pattern impression mat, spreading knife, small sharp knife, aspic cutters (optional), scissors, small plastic bag, toothpick

*Available at gourmet shops or through some mail order companies (see Resources, pages 183-186).

*Do not cut out the drawbridge; just score the outline of the drawbridge door into the dough.

Day One: Baking the Castle and Making the Accessories

1 Cut out the pattern.

2 Bake the Castle: Mix the gingerbread dough. Roll and cut the Castle pieces according to the directions on pages 16-18.

3 Dust the "stone" impression mat with powdered sugar and lay it firmly into the wall dough to create a stone look. Move to another section of the dough until the walls are completed.

4 Dust the "wood" impression mat with powdered sugar press into the remaining dough before cutting the drawbridge pattern.

5 Bake the Castle pieces according to the directions on pages 16 and 18.

6 Make the fondant flags: Knead yellow paste color into most of the fondant, red into the rest. Cut five flags following the pattern provided and drape them across the lollipop sticks so that they dry with curves. Cut five small stars from the red fondant and let dry. (I used aspic cutters.)

 TIP: *Remember to rest the tips of the decorating bags against damp paper towels between uses.*

Day Two: Assembling and Decorating

1 Attach the red fondant stars to the yellow fondant flags with dabs of icing. Attach the flags to the lollipop sticks. Let dry.

2 With the scissors, cut the sheet gelatin slightly larger than the window openings. Affix the sheet gelatin to the insides of the windows (not the sides with the "stone" impressions). Hold the sheet gelatin in place by icing the thin gingerbread strips over the edges. This will keep the windows from falling down inside of the castle after a month or two.

3 If desired, cover the board with foil.

4 Tint half of the icing brown and load it

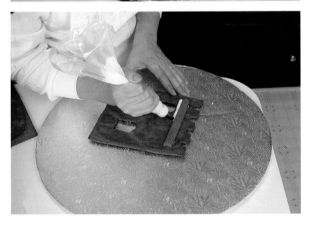

into one of the decorating bags with the coupler and #10 tip.

5 Ice the thick gingerbread roof support strips to the backs of the walls, approximately 3/4" from the top (see above photos). Reinforce with a thick bead of icing at the bottoms of these strips; they will be holding the roof up.

6 Assemble the four walls as instructed on pages 24 and 25. However, do not add the roof until they are completely dry (Step 15). Instead, work on the castle yard.

Note: See photo of the completed Castle for suggested yard item placement.

❼ With the spreading knife, spread a thin layer of white icing under the area where the moat is to go. Lay the drawbridge across the moat.

❽ Tint the piping gel blue and spread over the white icing.

❾ Put the #3 tip into the remaining decorating bag and load with 1 cup of white icing.

❿ Run a line of icing around the moat. Line with jellybeans. Run another line of icing over the jellybeans and add another layer of jellybeans.

⓫ Put the coconut into the plastic bag and add a large toothpick dab of green paste color. Roll it around in the bag until all the coconut is green. Set aside.

⓬ Tint the remaining icing green. With the knife, spread it all the way around the castle, leaving only the driveway area in front bare.

⓭ Press the green coconut into the green icing to create grass.

⓮ Spread a thin layer of brown icing on the driveway and press Grape Nuts in to create a gravel look.

⓯ Affix a flower to each caramel with icing and place them as pillars at the beginning of the driveway.

⓰ For the roof, run a thin line of icing along the tops of the supporting bars inside of the castle walls. Gently place the roof on top.

⓱ With the sharp knife, cut the tips off the ends of the ice cream sugar cones, making holes just large enough for the lollipop stick flagpoles to fit into. Ice the poles into place with brown icing.

⓲ Arrange the ice cream cone turrets on the roof of the castle, then ice them into place with brown icing and the #28 tip.

⓳ Affix the remaining flowers over the front door and windows.

⓴ Put a dab of icing underneath the dragon and put into place on the drawbridge.

Castle window strips
Make 12

Castle roof
Make 1

Enlarge 200%

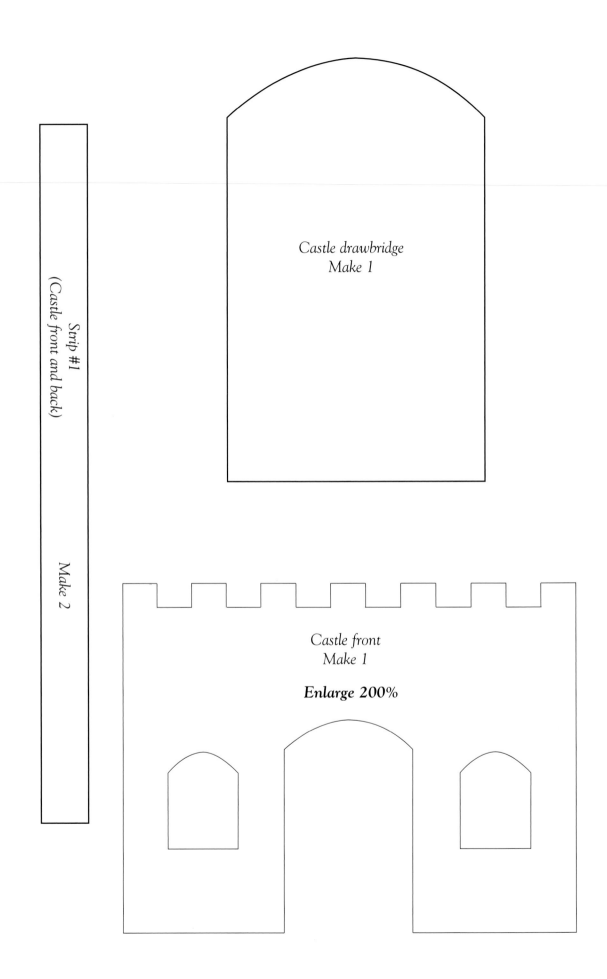

Strip #1
(Castle front and back)

Make 2

Castle drawbridge
Make 1

Castle front
Make 1

Enlarge 200%

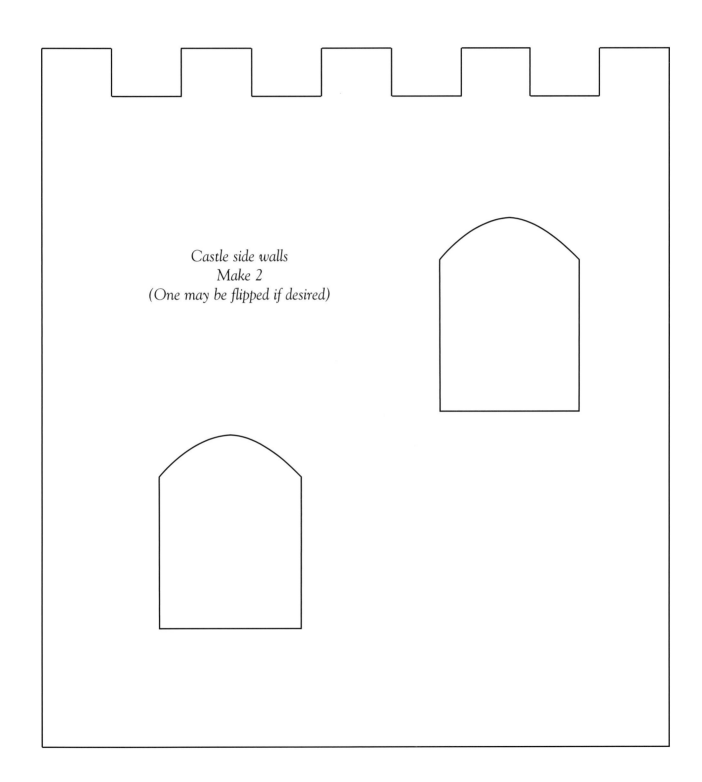

Strip #2 Castle sides
Make 2

Castle side walls
Make 2
(One may be flipped if desired)

Country Chapel

Difficulty Level: Moderately Easy

This country chapel, with its lights softly glowing through the stained glass windows, must be seen in person to truly be appreciated—photographs can't perfectly capture the beauty of the inside glow and the outside details at the same time. Adding to the allure of this particular structure is the fact that every single component is edible, from the delicate lace points at the top of the roof and the stunning stained glass windows, to the gravestones in the church-yard. It is truly a work of edible art.

Materials and Supplies

Copy of the pattern
Copy of the lace points
pattern (see page 47)
9" x 11" piece of cardboard
Board (16" circle or larger)
with a craft light attached
(see page 46 for instruc-
tions)
Foil, any color, if desired
1 batch basic gingerbread
recipe
1 batch royal icing
Powdered sugar

1/4 lb. fondant
4 sheets of sheet gelatin
3 ice cream sugar cones
Red cake decorating decors
2 silver dragees
2 cups shredded coconut
Approx. 14 almonds
Toasted coconut or Grape
Nuts cereal
4 decorating bags, 2 with
couplers
Tips #2, #3, #10, #16, #18,
and #32

Paste colors: assorted (for
stained glass windows),
green, brown, and gray
"Stone" pattern impression
mat, waxed paper, tape,
small paintbrush, rolling
pin, spreading knife, scissors, cup of water, ruler and
non-toxic pencil (optional)

Day One: Baking the Chapel and Making the Accessories

❶ Cut out the pattern.

❷ Make the Chapel: Mix the gingerbread dough. Roll, cut, and bake the Chapel according to the directions on pages 16-18. Do not cut out the front door, simply score the outline. Before cutting the chapel's stone walls, dust the impression mat with powdered sugar and firmly press it into the rolled dough. Carefully lift it up and cut the wall from the best part of the impression.

❸ Make lace points: Use the lace point pattern, cardboard, waxed paper, tape, icing, and a decorating bag with the #2 tip to make lace points according to the directions on page 45. (Although delicate and therefore easy to break when handling, they are also easy to make, and the sophisticated craftsmanship they add to your work is well worth the effort. Also, once they are on the gingerbread structure, they won't break unless bumped. Leftover lace points make fabulous additions to cakes and cookies, too, so don't worry about making too many, just too few.)

❹ Make the gravestones: Knead a small amount of gray paste color into the fondant, then roll flat. Cut a variety of gravestone shapes from the fondant between 1" and 2" tall.

❺ Paint the stained glass windows: First, with the scissors, cut the sheet gelatin down so that each window opening is covered, including a generous extension (approximately 1/2" beyond the frame all around). Then, using paste colors directly from the jars, paint each diamond on the sheet gelatin a different color. (Just rinse the paintbrush in the cup of water when you want to switch colors.)

❻ Make the trees: Tint 3 cups of the icing green. Load another decorating bag with green icing and the #32 tip. Squeeze icing against the bottom of one of the ice cream sugar cones. Stop squeezing and pull away to make a pine bough. Continue to make boughs all of the way around the bottom of the cone, then sprinkle with red decors. Continue to make each row of pine boughs in this manner, sprinkling with red decors after each row is completed. Create two additional trees in the same manner with the remaining cones.

❼ Let all pieces dry overnight. (Note: The gelatin windows won't completely dry for weeks to come, but they will be usable by the next day.)

 TIP: *Remember to rest the tips of the decorating bags against damp paper towels between uses.*

Day Two: Assembling and Decorating

❶ If desired, cover the board with foil.

❷ Tint half of the icing brown.

❸ Load one of the decorating bags with a coupler, brown icing, and #10 tip. Attach the "stained glass" gelatin windows to the insides of the window frames with small lines of icing. Then ice the small bars of gingerbread over the edges to hold them in place.

❹ Assemble the four walls and roof according to the directions on pages 24 and 25.

❺ Attach the buttresses to the side walls with small amounts of icing (see photo for placement). Reinforce the bottoms of the buttresses, where the brown icing will later be surrounded by "snow."

❻ Ice the steps to the front of the chapel, with the largest step on the bottom and the smallest step on the top.

Note: See photo of the completed Chapel for suggested icing and yard decoration placement.

7 Load the remaining decorating bag with a coupler, white icing, and #3 tip. Make a tile pattern on the roof. (To achieve an even pattern, I used a ruler and non-toxic pencil to mark off sections 1/2" wide x 1-1/4" long before applying icing.)

8 With the same decorating bag used in Step 6, trim the chapel with white icing with the following tips: #16 for the doors and windows, #18 for the side seams and under-hang (inserting one lace point onto the top front as you go), and #32 for the roof's peak.

9 After icing the roof's peak, immediately insert lace points into the roof trim.

10 Add the dragees to the front doors as doorknobs with small dots of icing.

11 With the spreading knife, spread a thick layer of white icing in the churchyard, one section at a time. Sprinkle with shredded coconut and insert gravestones and trees as you go.

12 Cut the tips off the ends of the almonds and line the sidewalk area with them. Then lightly press the toasted coconut or Grape Nuts into the snow to form a sidewalk.

13 Insert the stone walls into the edges of the snowy yard, reinforcing with white icing and the #10 tip, if necessary. Also, use the #10 tip to create a line of snow on top of the stone walls. Decorate the wall's seams with the #18 tip.

14 Lightly sprinkle the roof and front steps with powdered sugar.

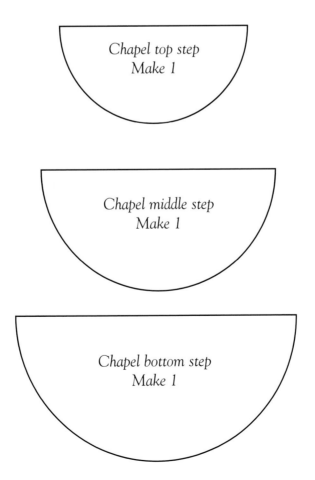

Chapel top step
Make 1

Chapel middle step
Make 1

Chapel bottom step
Make 1

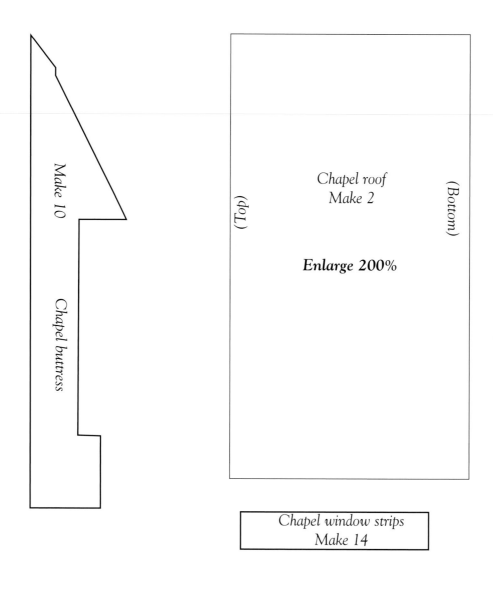

Make 10

Chapel buttress

Chapel roof
Make 2

(Top)

(Bottom)

Enlarge 200%

Chapel window strips
Make 14

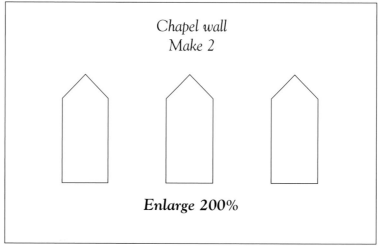

Chapel wall
Make 2

Enlarge 200%

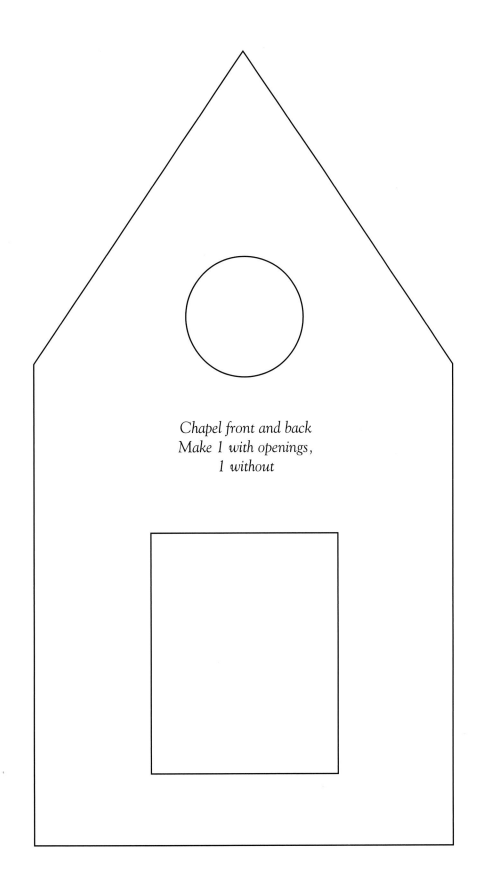

Chapel front and back
Make 1 with openings,
1 without

English Country Cottage

Difficulty Level: Easy

Imagine yourself biking along the backroads of merry old England. The roads are narrow but the scenery is beautiful, and every twist of the road brings a fresh surprise. When this charming cottage appears you just have to stop, rest, and soak it in. As John Keats said, "A thing of beauty is a joy forever."

Materials and Supplies

Copy of the pattern
Board (16" circle or larger)
Foil, any color, if desired
1 batch basic gingerbread recipe
1 batch royal icing
Powdered sugar
Shredded Wheat cereal

1/2 lb. jellybeans
1 tablespoon rice
1 silver dragee
Approx. 70 tiny pastel roses
Peanut brittle, cut into 1" squares
3 decorating bags, 1 with coupler

Tips: #10, #3, and #347
Paste colors: brown and green
"Stone" pattern impression mat, "wood" pattern impression mat, tray, spreading knife

Day One: Baking the Cottage

❶ Cut out the pattern.

❷ Make the Cottage: Mix the dough. Roll, cut, and bake the Cottage according to the directions on pages 16-18. However, before cutting, lightly dust the "stone" pattern impression mat with powdered sugar and press into the dough. Lift and repeat until a sufficient area is covered to make a wall. Lay down the pattern and cut. Also, dust the "wood" pattern impression mat with powdered sugar, press into the dough, lift, and cut the door.

❸ Make the chimney: Roll the remaining dough to approximately 1/2" thick, cut according to the pattern, and bake for approximately 30 minutes.

 TIP: *Remember to rest the tips of the decorating bags against damp paper towels between uses.*

Day Two: Assembling and Decorating

❶ If desired, cover the board with foil.

❷ Tint 2 cups of icing brown. Load into one of the decorating bags with the #10 tip. Assemble the house according to the directions on pages 24 and 25.

❸ Still with the brown icing, attach the chimney to the side of the house and the door to the front of the house.

❹ Over a tray for easy clean-up, break the Shredded Wheat into clumps and strands. Again, with brown icing, attach the Shredded Wheat to the roof, beginning at the bottom and working your way up.

❺ Load 1 cup of white icing into another decorating bag with the (washed and dried) #10 tip.

❻ Cover 1" of the chimney at a time with white icing and affix jellybeans. Proceed until the chimney is finished.

❼ Pipe white icing in front of the door to form a sidewalk. Cover with rice for gravel.

❽ Add the silver dragee to the front door as a doorknob.

❾ Tint the remaining icing soft green and load into the remaining decorating bag with the coupler and #3 tip.

Note: See photo of the completed Cottage for suggested vine and rose placement.

❿ Make vines where the roses are to be placed: above the door, along the window sills, climbing up walls.

⓫ Change the decorating bag with green icing to the #347 tip. Attach roses, reserving some for Step 12, and secure with leaves.

⓬ Using the spreading knife, ice the yard around the house with green icing, laying the peanut brittle as a stone wall as you go.

⓭ With green icing and the #347 tip, affix the remaining roses to the wall.

Enlarge 200%

Cottage chimney
Make 1 very thick

(Top)

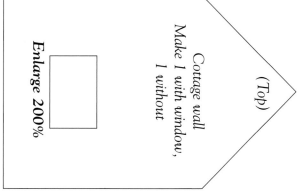

Enlarge 200%

Cottage wall
Make 1 with window,
1 without

(Top)

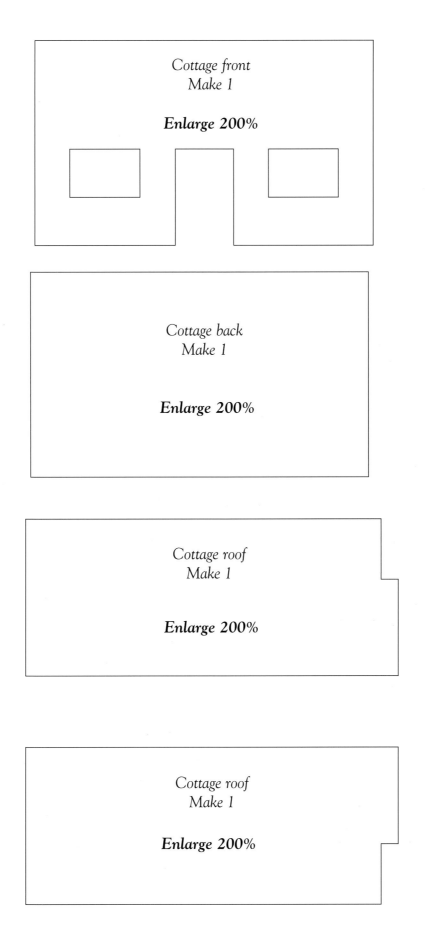

Cottage front
Make 1

Enlarge 200%

Cottage back
Make 1

Enlarge 200%

Cottage roof
Make 1

Enlarge 200%

Cottage roof
Make 1

Enlarge 200%

Southwestern Ranch House

Difficulty Level: Easy

This simple adobe ranch, with its chili pepper Christmas trees and decorated cacti, is my husband's favorite gingerbread house. This is especially endearing to me because he hails from Athens, Greece, and doesn't have a drop of the southwest in his blood. However, he likes how the feeling of a desert dwelling is captured in a medium usually reserved for country cottages and old Victorians.

Materials and Supplies

Copy of the pattern
Board (14" circle or larger)
Foil, any color, if desired
1 batch basic gingerbread recipe
1 batch royal icing
Cacti cookie cutter*
2" ball of fondant
Powdered sugar

1 lasagna noodle
3 small pretzel sticks
1 lb. red licorice nibs
1 tablespoon colored dragees
6 chili peppers
1-1/2 cups brown sugar
1 tablespoon cornstarch
2 decorating bags

Tips: #10 and #2
Paste colors: green, brown, and red
"Wood" pattern impression mat, spreading knife, medium-sized paintbrush

*Cookies can be made from either gingerbread or sugar cookie dough.

Day One: Baking the Ranch House and Making the Door

1 Cut out the pattern.

2 Bake the house: Mix the gingerbread dough. Roll, cut, and bake the Ranch House according to the directions on pages 16-18. Also make the cacti, either from sugar cookie dough or gingerbread, at this time.

3 Make the door: Work a little red paste color into the fondant. Dust your work surface and the impression mat with powdered sugar. Press the mat into the fondant. Lift and cut out the door.

4 Cut a small red star approximately 1/4" tall for above the entryway.

5 Let all pieces harden overnight.

 TIP: Remember to rest the tips of the decorating bags against damp paper towels between uses.

Early in Day Two: Whitewashing the Walls

1 Prepare a color flow whitewash: Add water, 1/2 teaspoon at a time, to 1 cup of white icing. It will have achieved proper consistency when a drop of icing, dripped back into the bowl, has totally blended in by the count of six.

2 With the paintbrush, paint the four house walls and the three front yard walls white. Also paint the edges of the roof white, for they will show after the tiles have been attached.

 TIP: See page 12 for instructions on making a Poor Person's Drying Table.

3 Leave to dry for several hours.

Later in Day Two: Assembling and Decorating

4 If desired, cover the board with foil.

5 Load one of the decorating bags with white icing and the #10 tip. With your hands, break the lasagna noodle into 1" pieces. Use the white icing to attach them to the insides of the window frames.

6 Insert small, even pretzel stick pieces into the holes above the front windows. Ice into place.

7 Assemble the house according to the directions on pages 24 and 25. (Do not add the front yard walls until Step 15.)

8 Ice the red licorice to the roof with white icing and the #10 tip. Begin at the bottom of the roof and work your way up.

9 When you've tiled both sides of the roof, top it off with a row of red licorice lying lengthwise.

10 Attach the fondant front door to the front of the house and a dragee as the doorknob.

11 Tint 1/4 cup of the icing green. Load the icing into the remaining decorating bag and the #2 tip and make prickles on the cacti.

12 With the green icing, affix dragees to the cacti and chili peppers to look like ornaments.

13 Tint the rest of the icing light brown.

14 Mix the cornstarch with the brown sugar.

15 Spread brown icing in the front yard. Then sprinkle with brown sugar mixture and press into icing, reserving some for Step 17.

16 Attach the front yard walls to the front of the house with white icing.

17 Affix the red star above the entryway.

Note: See photo of the completed Ranch House for suggested yard decoration placement.

18 Finish the yard: Spread brown icing around the house and cover with the remaining brown sugar mixture. Decorate the yard with the chili pepper trees and cookie cacti you made in Step 11 as you go.

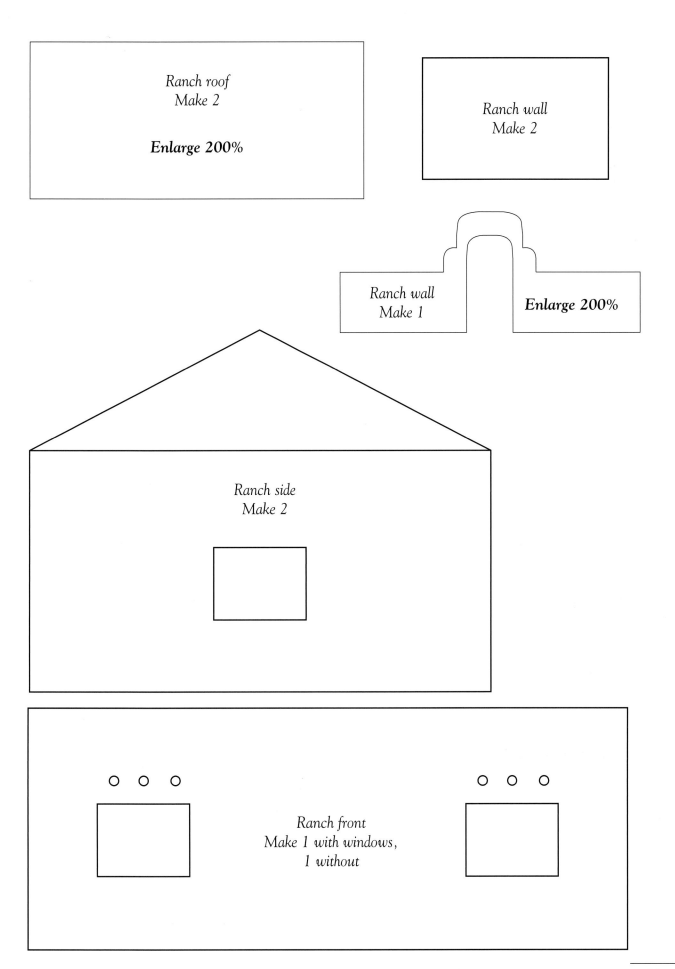

Ranch roof
Make 2

Enlarge 200%

Ranch wall
Make 2

Ranch wall
Make 1

Enlarge 200%

Ranch side
Make 2

Ranch front
Make 1 with windows,
1 without

Suburban Split-level

Difficulty Level: Moderately Challenging

Who says that classic Victorian gingerbread houses are the only way to celebrate Christmas? Santa's sleigh sails into the suburbs, too! Here the family eagerly awaits the jolly one on his special day with decorative displays all over the yard. Just as these suburban split-level houses are often pre-fabricated and mass-produced (although endearingly personalized!), I have used pre-fabricated, mass-produced cake decorations to decorate it. Not only is it easy and fun to do, it is one of the children's very favorites.

Materials and Supplies

Copy of the pattern
Board (12" x 18" or larger)
Foil, any color, if desired
Piece of 3/4" thick craft Styrofoam
1 batch basic gingerbread recipe
1 batch royal icing
1/2 lb. fondant
Powdered sugar

1 basketball net cake decoration
1 lollipop stick
1 box Nabisco Sweet Crispers
Many ready-made decorations*
1/2 cup Tart & Tinys
10 caramels
1 cup pretzel sticks

Alphabet pasta**
1 decorating bag with coupler
Tips: #3, #10, #16, and #21
Paste colors: black or gray
Rolling pin, spreading knife

*You will need decorations for the house, roof, fence, and yard.
**See Day Two, Step 18, for needed numbers.

Swiss Chalet

Difficulty Level: Easy

This Swiss mountain retreat is my favorite house. I can easily envision a happy family inside, clad in Nordic sweaters, laughing and drinking hot chocolate after a long day of skiing.

Materials and Supplies

Copy of the pattern
Board (16" circle or larger)
Foil, any color, if desired
1-1/2 batches basic gingerbread recipe
2 batches royal icing
1 ice cream sugar cone
Cake decorating decors
1/2 foot of lace trim
12 candles*
1 large wreath*

2 small wreaths*
4 bells*
Approx. 10 small dragees
Approx. 65 large silver dragees (I used 63)
3/4 lb. large colored nonpariels
1 cup of coconut flakes**
8 square Jolly Rancher candies
3 decorating bags and 2

couplers
Tips: #3,#10, #16, #32, #104, and #349
Paste color: green
Spreading knife, waxed paper

*These items were purchased ready-made at a cake decorating store.
**I used desiccated coconut from a local cake decorating store for the soft, non-shiny look.

Day One: Baking the Chalet and Making the Accessories

1 Cut out the pattern.

2 Make the Chalet: Mix the gingerbread dough. Roll, cut, and bake the Chalet pieces according to the directions on pages 16-18.

3 Make the trees: Tint 2 cups of the icing green. Load one of the decorating bags with a coupler, the #16 tip, and green icing. Starting at the bottom of the ice cream sugar cone, squeeze the icing against the cone, stop squeezing, and pull away. This will form a pine bough. Continue forming boughs around the tree. After each row is completed, sprinkle with decors.

4 Make the bushes: Change to the #32 tip. Form a 1" to 1-1/2" green icing circle on waxed paper and proceed in one continuous stroke, getting smaller and smaller until a bush is formed. Sprinkle immediately with cake decorating decors. Make a total of seven bushes.

5 Let all pieces dry overnight.

 TIP: *Remember to rest the tips of the decorating bags against damp paper towels between uses.*

Day Two: Assembling and Decorating

1 If desired, cover the board with foil.

2 Cut the lace trim into 2" pieces and ice to the insides of each window with small dabs of white icing.

3 Assemble the four walls and roof according to the directions on pages 24 and 25.

4 Load one of the decorating bags with a coupler, white icing, and the #104 tip. With the wide end up, tilt the tip slightly outward and pipe half a heart onto each shutter. Tilt the tip in the opposite direction and form the other heart halves.

5 With white icing, affix two shutters around each window and attach the front door.

6 Ice the candles in the windows. Icing may be used to attach the candles to the curtains for extra support.

7 Attach the balcony sides to the back of the balcony at the ends (laying them down flat). Then position the balcony above the front door, obscuring the second floor windows a little bit.

Note: See photo of the completed Chalet for suggested decoration placement.

8 Affix the wreaths and bells to the front of the house.

9 Load the final decorating bag with green icing and the #349 tip. Make a series of leaves on the balcony to form garland. Add small silver dragees, reserving one for the next step.

10 Affix one dragee as a doorknob to the front door.

11 With the spreading knife and white icing, lightly ice half of the roof. Place the colored non-pariels in even rows, beginning at the bottom and working your way up the roof. Complete the other half of the roof in the same manner.

12 Switch the tip on the decorating bag with white icing to the #32 and add a star border to the edges of the roof. Top each star with a large silver dragee.

13 Still with the #32 tip, make stars up the side seams.

14 Switch to the #10 tip and form icicles around the roof's underhang.

15 Using the spreading knife, ice the yard with the remaining white icing, sprinkling with coconut and the placing trees and bushes as you go.

16 Lay the Jolly Rancher squares in front of the house as a sidewalk.

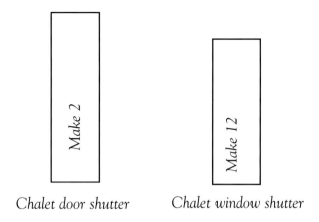

Chalet door shutter   *Chalet window shutter*

Make 2

Make 12

Chalet side wall
Make 2

Chalet roof
Make 2

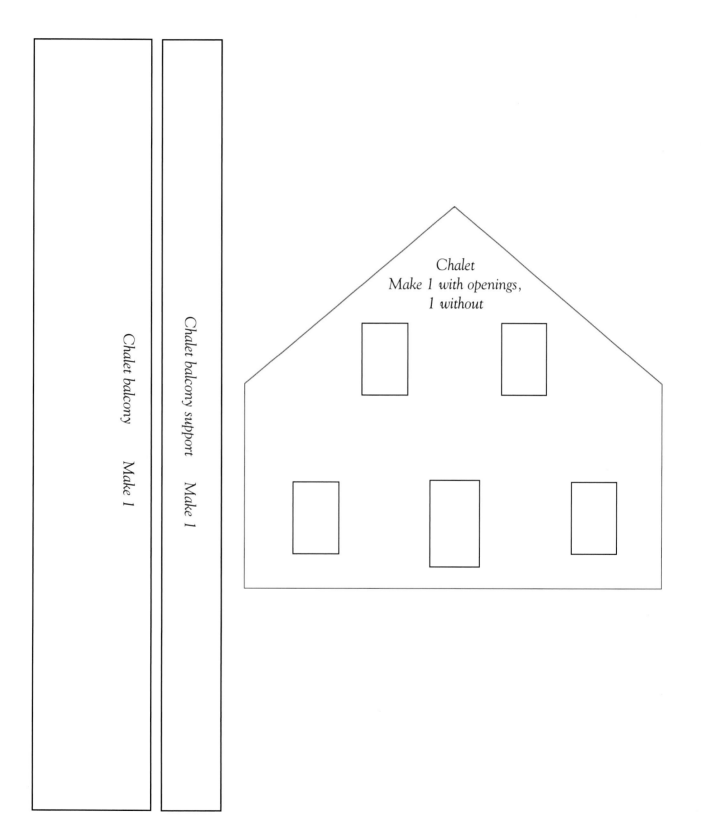

Chalet balcony   Make 1

Chalet balcony support   Make 1

Chalet
Make 1 with openings,
1 without

Victorian

This simple, traditional Victorian house whispers Christmas in a way that no other gingerbread house can. From the gentle candles glowing in the windows, to the wreath and welcome mat at the front door, the essence of holiday happiness and family togetherness resonates from this house.

This particular home hails from the South, where snow and frost are not likely to be found on Christmas Day. However, with a little powdered sugar on the roof and white icing in the yard, the peaceful scene is magically transported into the North.

Materials and Supplies

Copy of the pattern
Board (16" circle or larger)
Foil, any color, if desired
1 batch basic gingerbread recipe
1-1/2 batches royal icing
1 lb. fondant
Powdered sugar
1/4 lb. white candy melts
1 rectangular cookie
9 candles*
1 large wreath*

1 small wreath*
Alphabet pasta**
5 caramels
Fresh thyme sprigs
Fresh rosemary
1 decorating bag with coupler
Tips: #10, #18, #32, and #21 (optional)
Paste colors: Wedgwood blue, brown, pink, and forest green

Garrett Frill Cutter, rolling pin, serrated rolling pin, small sharp knife, fence mold, spoon, small paintbrush, spreading knife

*These items were purchased ready-made at a cake-decorating store.
**See Day One, Step 8 for needed letters.

Day One: Baking the Victorian and Making the Accessories

❶ Cut out the pattern.

❷ Make the Victorian: Mix the gingerbread dough. Roll, cut, and bake the Victorian pieces according to the directions on pages 16-18. Take care when making the front porch: Cut out the inside lines first, then the outside lines. This piece will be weak when warm, so try not to move it until completely cooled. You may want to make two in case one breaks.

❸ Make the roof tiles: Color three-quarters of the fondant Wedgwood blue and leave the rest white.

❹ Sprinkle your work space with powdered sugar. Working quickly with only small amounts of fondant at a time, roll it out. Cut long pieces with the Garrett Frill Cutter, then divide the long sections into smaller pieces. (I made most of mine four ruffles long with an occasional three-, two-, and one-ruffle piece to fill gaps, as shown here.) Make about ninety roof tiles.

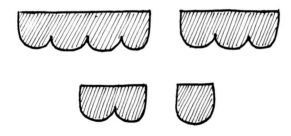

TIP: *Keep all unused fondant tightly wrapped in plastic.*

TIP: *Remember to rest the tip of the decorating bag against a damp paper towel between uses.*

❺ Make the shutters: Sprinkle your work surface with powdered sugar and roll out the remaining blue fondant with the serrated rolling pin. Make eighteen 1-1/2" x 3-1/3" shutters (two for each window).

❻ Make the crossbars: Sprinkle your work surface with powdered sugar and roll out the white fondant. With the small sharp knife, cut nine 2" x 2-1/2" crossbars for the windows.

❼ Make the candy melt fence: Heat the candy melts in a microwave, stirring every 30 seconds or until completely melted. Spoon into the fence mold and freeze or refrigerate until firm (see Candy Melts, page 30).

❽ Make the welcome mat: Thin some icing with water and color it with a small amount of pink paste color. Paint it on the rectangular cookie and add desired words with alphabet pasta.

❾ Let welcome mat and all fondant pieces harden overnight.

Day Two: Assembling and Decorating

❶ If desired, cover the board with foil.

❷ Load the decorating bag with brown icing, the coupler, and #10 tip.

❸ Attach the white fondant cross bars to the inside of the windows with large dots of icing.

❹ Continuing with the brown icing, assemble the house according to the directions on pages 24 and 25.

❺ Attach the sides of the gable, on the top front roof.

Note: See photo of the completed Victorian for suggested decoration placement.

❻ Attach the front door, as well as any other decorations you want inside of the front porch (including the candles in the windows).

7 Ice the front porch's floor to the cake board. Add the welcome mat. Attach the sides and front of your porch, adding the roof last.

8 Starting on the front of the house, tile the roof. Begin attaching fondant tiles with dabs of brown icing at the bottom of the gable, working your way up to complete the gable. Do the rest of the front roof in the same manner.

9 Tile the porch roof with brown icing and blue fondant roof tiles. Again, begin at the bottom and work your way up.

10 Tile the back roof with brown icing and blue fondant roof tiles.

11 Attach candles to the crossbars of the remaining windows and the large wreath to the front of the gable.

12 Switch to the #32 tip and decoratively reinforce the seams all around the house with a shell border, as seen in the photo. (The star pattern on the top of the front porch was done with a #21.)

13 Cut the caramels in half with the small sharp knife to make sidewalk squares.

14 Tint several cups of icing forest green. With the spreading knife, begin icing the front yard in a thick layer. Insert fresh thyme in front of the porch. Lay the caramels as a sidewalk and position the candy melt fence around them, in front of the house. If anything begins to tip over, lift it up, apply more icing, and reinsert.

15 Finish icing the rest of the yard in a thick layer, adding fresh rosemary for trees as you go.

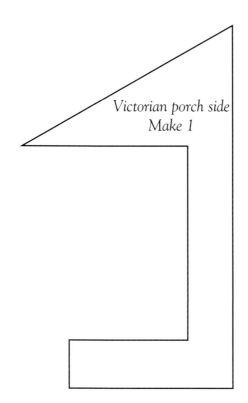

Victorian porch side
Make 1

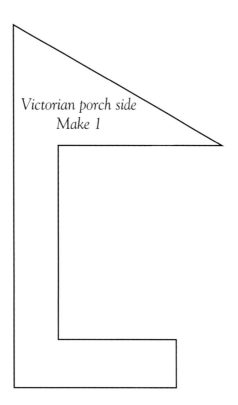

Victorian porch side
Make 1

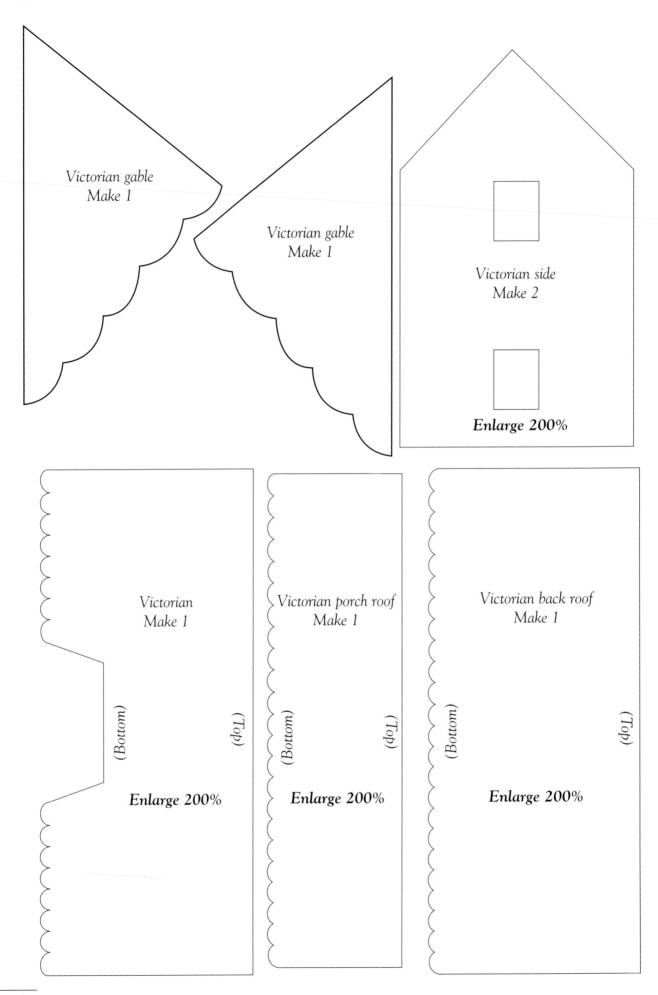

Victorian gable
Make 1

Victorian gable
Make 1

Victorian side
Make 2

Enlarge 200%

Victorian
Make 1

(Bottom)

(Top)

Enlarge 200%

Victorian porch roof
Make 1

(Bottom)

(Top)

Enlarge 200%

Victorian back roof
Make 1

(Bottom)

(Top)

Enlarge 200%

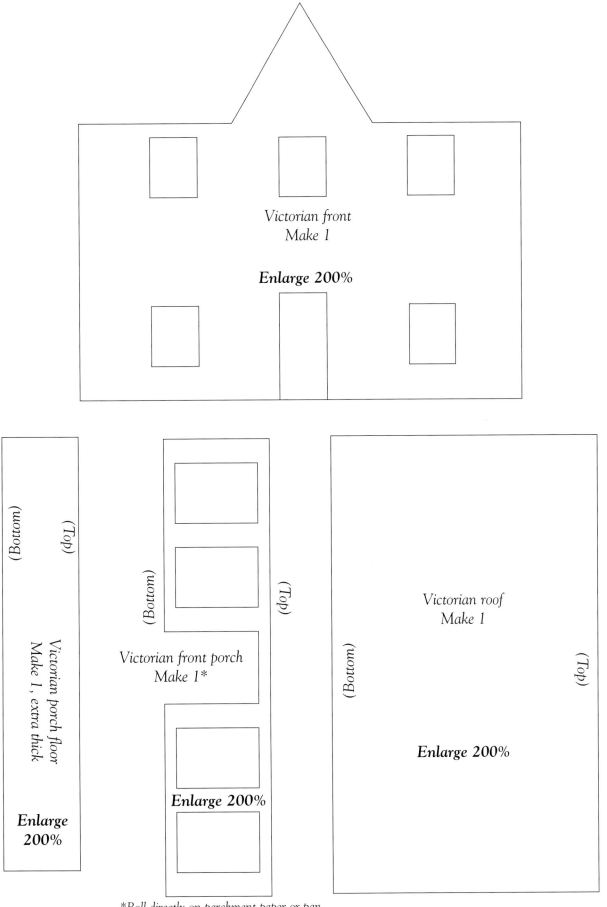

Victorian front
Make 1

Enlarge 200%

(Bottom) (Top)

Victorian porch floor
Make 1, extra thick

**Enlarge
200%**

(Bottom) (Top)

Victorian front porch
Make 1*

Enlarge 200%

(Bottom) (Top)

Victorian roof
Make 1

Enlarge 200%

*Roll directly on parchment paper or pan.
It cannot be moved before baking

Gingerbread Chips

Roll out leftover gingerbread dough and cut it into 1" strips. Cut these strips into small 1" squares. Bake at 350° for 5 to 7 minutes. When cooled, place these gingerbread chips in a bowl next to your gingerbread house so that snackers can enjoy the delicious taste of gingerbread while keeping their hands off of your house!

Gingerbread chips are quick and easy to make!

Gingerbread People

Making gingerbread people from leftover dough hardly needs to be mentioned, yet it cannot be left off of this list, either. Everyone loves gingerbread people!

Gingerbread boys and girls have been popular cookies for centuries.

Miniature Houses

Once you have made a big gingerbread house, little ones are a piece of cake! They can be used as ornaments or simply small decorations. (Note: The bottom piece is only necessary if you are going to hang them as ornaments. Then you must also attach a loop of ribbon with royal icing.)

Bake the pieces according to the baking instructions on page 16 for 8 to 10 minutes. Assemble them according to the standard assembly instructions on pages 24 and 25. However, instead of using a wooden base to rest your house on, you will be using a gingerbread base.

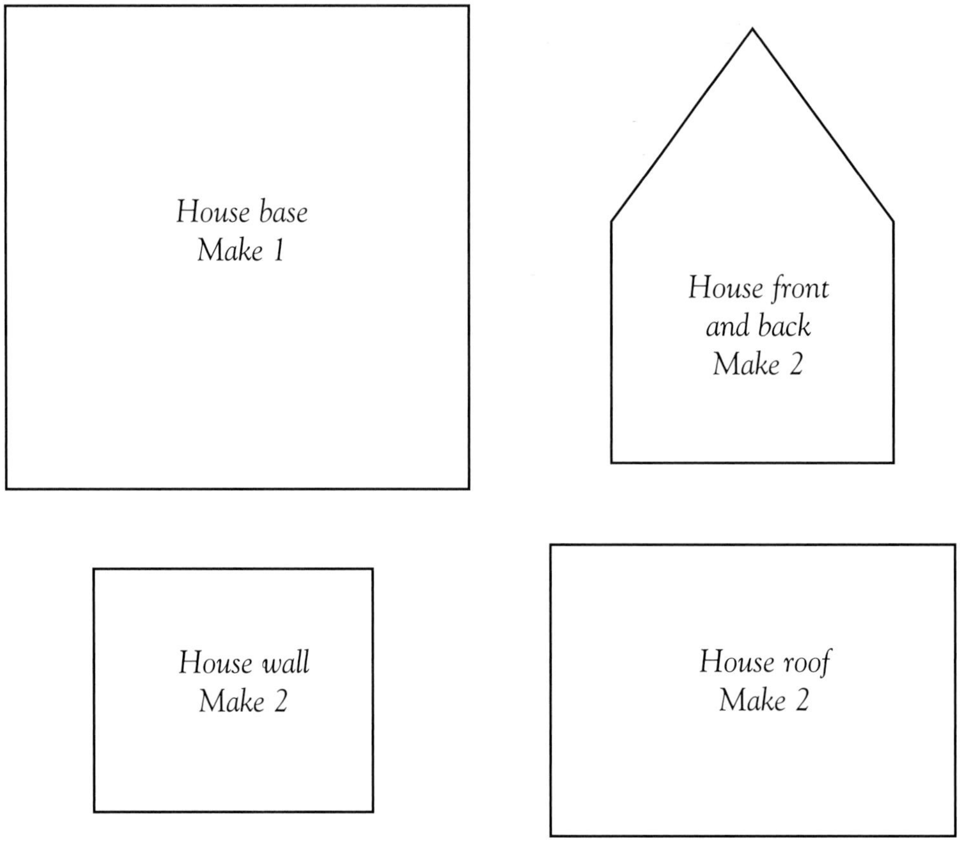

House base
Make 1

House front
and back
Make 2

House wall
Make 2

House roof
Make 2

Chapter 6

To Eat It or Save It? That is the Question!

The big day for eating the gingerbread house has finally arrived!

Sometimes the biggest question at the end of the holiday season isn't when to take down the Christmas tree or what to do with the sweater Aunt Mary gave you—it's whether or not to eat the gingerbread house. After all, you put so much work in to the project, and it *did* come out looking gorgeous, so how could you possibly eat it? Yet, is it worth the effort to save it? Won't the colors fade and the decorations fall? Will the walls crumble? Let the following information help you decide.

Gingerbread houses can be stored for up to three years in the driest parts of the country. (Some houses have been saved for even longer, but only as shadows of their former selves.) In places like Arizona and New Mexico, the prospects for saving your gingerbread house are good if it is stored properly. More humid areas, like St. Louis and Seattle,

make the prospect of saving it more of a challenge. In either case, it will never look as bright and as fresh as it did that first year (it is made of food, after all). Some decorations may even need to be reattached with fresh royal icing. The main structure, however, should be sound and sturdy, so it might be worth a try.

A small jar of Blue Ice will help wick moisture away from your gingerbread house. For product and availability information (see Resources, page 185).

Guidelines:

- **Do not** wrap the gingerbread house in plastic. Moisture will accumulate and the walls will collapse.
- **Do** store the house in a cardboard box to keep dust from settling on it.
- **Do** place the box in an interior closet of your house where it is least likely to suffer large fluctuations in temperature.
- **Do not** store it in an attic or basement where there are extreme ranges in temperature.
- **Do** place a drying agent in the box along with your gingerbread house to help absorb moisture, your biggest enemy.

If you decide to consume your gingerbread house (a practice I both recommend and follow for this edible art), then it may help to have a small ritual to say goodbye to your masterpiece. On either New Year's Eve or New Year's Day, gather your friends and family around, place the gingerbread house in the middle of the group, and read the following poem. It's the perfect way to say goodbye to your sweet house and hello to the year ahead.

Do you want to make a permanent holiday house? One woman poured concrete into her chocolate molds. When the pieces were dry she glued them together with Liquid Nails!

New Year's Poem for Eating Your Gingerbread House

Eating this house so fair and sweet
Brings insight to the year you'll meet.
For every bite has a tale to tell,
So eat for luck and wish you well.

If the front door is your choice to eat,
Far-flung visitors soon you'll greet.
But if on the pathway you choose to dine,
A trip afar will soon be thine.

Consume the roof if you want security,
For love and shelter will be a surety.
Tho' if it's adventure to which you aspire,
Devour the windows to achieve your desire.

From the warmth of the chimney true love will come;
A taste of it and a pair you'll become.
Or if, by chance, you're already a pair,
Eating the chimney will recharge the air.

Trees and bushes bring money your way,
While lawn decorations bring laughter and play.
Fences bring projects at which you'll succeed,
And people bring kindness and help when there's need.

But indulge in some pieces that aren't mentioned here,
You'll have special surprises throughout the New Year.

Happy New Year!

Nonnie Cargas, *Gingerbread Houses: Baking and Building Memories*, Krause Publications, 1999.

Chapter 7
Sharing the Joy

While some hobbies provide an outlet for frustration or the chance to make a statement, I believe gingerbread is a hobby that's just for fun. Oh sure, kneading the dough, baking the pieces, and constructing the houses can be therapeutic, and yes, each creation expresses the taste and interests of its creator, but the main reason people make gingerbread houses is to bring joy to themselves and those around them. Then, when the gingerbread bakers see the delight one house can bring to family and friends, they often want to share their talents with the larger community. That's what this chapter is for. I've been involved with contests and donations and am happy to share what I've learned. There is a great deal of satisfaction that comes with sharing your talents and interests with others, and this chapter will hopefully help pave the way to a successful event. Gingerbread holds universal appeal, and gingerbread events can't help but be rewarding for all involved.

How to Throw a Gingerbread Party

A gingerbread house raising may take a little more planning than your average holiday party, but the results are well worth the effort. This is the type of party that everyone wants to be invited to, young and old alike, craft lovers, and the not-particularly handy. The guidelines below provide general planning tips for any host or hostess, with specific ideas for children in the paragraphs that follow.

Brown bags are perfect to make gingerbread party invitations.

Before the Party:

• **Decide** where to have it and whom to invite. Remember that gingerbread decorators need a lot of room to spread out, so plan accordingly. Three to five guests is usually a good number.

• **Invite** your family and friends. I have found that 1-1/2 to 2 hours is a good length of time for children, but three or more is better for adults (especially craft lovers, who tend to want to do a good, careful job).

• **Gather** your materials and supplies. If inexpensive disposable decorating bags are unavailable, you can provide knives with small bowls of royal icing for each guest. Remember to keep them covered with a damp cloth when not in use.

• **Prepare** your houses. With young children you will probably want to assemble them before the party (consider using graham crackers as explained on page 40), but older children and adults enjoy assembling their own.

On the Day of the Party:

* **Assemble** each guest's supplies at his or her place at the table. Shared materials, like candy and pretzels, can be put on plates or platters that are passed around as needed.
* **Provide** drinks, but not too many munchies. Most people will be too absorbed in the project to eat and they snack on the candy and cookie decorations anyway!
* **Play** festive Christmas music. That way all five senses are incorporated into your holiday party: the sound of the music, the feel of the craft, the smell of the gingerbread, the sight of the houses, and the taste of the sweets!
* **Enjoy** yourself. A host's or hostess' happiness and enthusiasm are contagious!

A gingerbread party can be thrown for children as young as three years of age if the houses are assembled and left to dry before the children arrive. Well-constructed houses will withstand even the heavy, uncoordinated pressure of pre-schoolers. Some young guests and even older children may not appreciate the extra effort that homebaked gingerbread houses require, so go ahead and make graham cracker houses for the big day!

The only other differences between parties for children and parties for adults are the amount of time and assistance kids may need. Small children probably need an adult for every three or four of them, although with older kids this is unnecessary. All children, however, tend to work much more quickly than adults do, though, so you might want to have a plan for those that finish early. You can just have them run off to play or you could provide additional cookies for more decorating fun. Even plain old graham crackers can be made into edible gift tags or mini canvasses for their artistic creations.

Quick Fact: The term "gingerbread" can accurately be used to describe everything from ornately decorated houses to spiced fruit cakes, yeasted sweet loaves, and tea breads, to chunky cookies and moist, sticky cakes.

How to Enter a Gingerbread Contest

When entering a gingerbread contest it is important to remember that judges are as individual in their likes, dislikes, and opinions as are the people entering the show. One person's second place may be another's Best of Show. Admittedly, sometimes a house is entered that clearly stands apart from the rest, but just as often the final decision comes down to a matter of personal preference on the part of the judge(s). With that in mind, read through the following list of judging criteria, try to meet the goals as best you can, and be sure to enjoy yourself as you bake, build, decorate, and enter your project. Never lose sight of the joy that gingerbread is meant to bring.

 TIP: *For more information, see How to Sponsor a Gingerbread Contest on the next page.*

❶ Is the gingerbread evenly baked? Judges look for level walls and even thicknesses throughout the structure. A little browning at the edges of the house is acceptable, but it should not be burnt.

❷ Is the structure well-built? Walls should be as straight as possible, roofs should not sag, and chimney pieces need to be aligned.

❸ Are all of the decorations edible? In most contests, points are deducted for non edible decorations, such as plastic sleighs and foam trees. Others allow them, but grant additional points for edible decorations. Read the contest rules carefully and when in doubt, leave non-edibles out.

❹ Is the overall design attractive? The house needs to have a cohesive, balanced look based on a good idea. The plan does not have to be original unless specifically stated in the rules.

❺ Is the work neat? Well-placed decorations formed with the proper tools will always earn higher points than sloppy decorations created with makeshift equipment.

It is perfectly acceptable to enter your gingerbread house in more than one contest, but most of them are held simultaneously during the holiday season. When that's over, look for local cake shows; many of them have a gingerbread category, but they often stipulate that the project must be made within one year of the show.

Good luck and enjoy the contest!

Quick Fact: Ground ginger is derived from gingerroot, the fibrous, woody root of a tropical plant. Crystallized ginger is fresh gingerroot that has been cooked in sugar syrup and coated with granulated sugar.

How to Sponsor a Gingerbread Contest

Gingerbread contests are easy to plan, exciting to execute, and fun to attend. Held alone, or as part of a larger program such as a holiday bazaar, gingerbread contests are a sure way to attract young and old alike. Indeed, they are usually one of the main attractions of a winter event.

There are six things to consider when planning a gingerbread contest. They are: advertising; rules and regulations; registration and entry fees; certificates, ribbons, and awards; arrival and set-up of entries; and judging.

In order to have a successful contest, you will probably want to feature at least fifteen houses. To attract this many houses, you need to spread the word everywhere. For example, if you are doing this as a church project, just notifying the members of your parish may not be enough. Even though there may be five hundred families in the parish, the vast majority is interested in seeing the results of the contest rather than entering it. You need to spread the word out into the community. Put signs up in schools, grocery stores, and all types of craft stores. Attach official rules and entry forms to the signs, or inform the public where they can be obtained by providing a phone number and address.

The official rules and regulations will vary from contest to contest, but all contain some specific information. What are the categories? When are the entrants supposed to drop off their creations? When are awards distributed? When are the people allowed to take their entries home? A sample of a form I wrote for an actual gingerbread contest at our local farm museum is provided on pages 135 and 136 for you to peruse. Feel free to use the rules that fit your particular group or situation and modify or eliminate those that don't.

Having your contestants pre-register helps you plan for the number of entries that will be arriving on the day of the contest (so you can set up the correct number of tables, etc.). However, requiring contestants to pre-register

discourages some last-minute entries. The idea my cake club came up with to encourage pre-registration, without requiring it, was simple yet effective: give an early bird discount. To those people who mail in their entry fees before the day of the show, a $2 discount is given, so they pay $3 to enter. Those registering the day of the show pay $5. This helps those gingerbread crafters who want to wait until they see if their house turned out well the night before the contest feel comfortable.

The entry fees are used to pay for the next part of the planning process, which is obtaining certificates, ribbons, and awards. Some contests, especially if they are affiliated with a cake decorating store, also offer prizes such as cake pans. While nice, I often find these prizes to be unnecessary. Your average contestant is primarily interested in recognition of his or her talent. A beautiful First Place ribbon, or even silver cup for Best of Show, is the most tangible and traditional recognition of these talents. All contestants should be given a certificate of participation (easily made on a computer) and Honorable Mentions should be awarded liberally. I am also a strong proponent of People's Choice awards. These not only enable you to broaden your range of prizewinners, but they also directly involve the public with the contest.

Just be sure to divide the People's Choice awards into categories. It's unfair to pit a 10-year-old from the children's group against an experienced decorator.

Although one or two organized individuals can easily handle the arrangement of the contest, if it's a large contest you might want to have several more people on hand when entries are due to arrive. First, tables need to be set up and covered. Then, when the contestants come, entry fees and forms must be taken and numbers assigned. Allow each contestant to set up his or her house in the assigned spot and try to move them as little as possible. Also, rope off the displays to prohibit the public from coming too close and touching them. Many contest organizers like to set out a big bowl of inexpensive candy near the People's Choice ballot box so that the people who *have* to snack aren't tempted by someone's entry.

Judging should be done during a lull in the festivities or before or after the show opens for the day. Three judges are recommended in case there is a tie on any of the entries. Suggested people for this job include professional bakers, experienced decorators, cake shop owners, cake decorating judges, and others from the world of food, pastries, and cake decorating. You might also want to include the church pastor, nursing home administrator, or other sponsor of the event. People willing to be judges are not hard to find; just look for those whose judgment your contestants will respect.

What should judges look for in the way of winning entries? Like any other contest decision, some of the assessment is a matter of personal taste. However, there are some specific things that matter in the world of gingerbread. First, how are the pieces baked? Are they a nice, even color and of uniform thickness throughout? How detailed are they? Is the same technique used over and over, or has the creator used a variety of ideas and methods in the execution of the house? Does it seem original or unique? What is the overall impression—neat and clever or sloppy and uninspired? Keep in mind, too, the levity of these contests, as opposed to gravity. Gingerbread contests are primarily for fun. Be kind. No one needs his or her feelings hurt (especially if you are using comment cards, as are frequently given in cake decorating contests). And, if in doubt, be generous. Ribbons are cheap compared to the happiness they can bestow upon some hard-working craftsperson.

Tips:
- **Do** put the gingerbread creations on displays where they are all easily seen.
- **Do** use single-color tablecloths; patterns and multiple colors are distracting.
- **Do** rope off the area, keeping spectators several feet away from the houses. (People *will* touch and nibble, given the chance.)
- **Don't** over-decorate the area around the houses. Keep the focus on the crafts.

 TIP: Consider providing a big bowl of inexpensive candy for the spectators to munch on. It cuts down on gingerbread thievery considerably!

A Sample of Contest Rules

Farm Museum Gingerbread Contest Official Rules and Regulations

① Design and bake a gingerbread creation to fit one of the four categories listed below.

② Enter the contest by bringing your creation, completed entry form, and $4.00 entry fee to the Farm Museum on Friday, December 5, 1998, between the hours of 10:00 a.m. and 4:00 p.m. Contestants may enter more than one creation, but each entry must be accompanied by its own entry form and fee.

③ Entries will be judged on Saturday, December 6. Ribbons will be awarded at 3:00 p.m., but designers need not be present to win.

④ Entries will be displayed at the Farm Museum from December 5 through the 13. All entries must be picked up between 5:00 p.m. and 8:00 p.m. on Sunday, December 13, but not before that time because they will be part of the museum's advertised display.

⑤ Houses must be constructed primarily of gingerbread and icing. Non-visible support structures may be used.

⑥ The judges reserve the right to place the gingerbread creations in the most appropriate categories. All decisions are final.

⑦ Due to the age of the building, electricity is not available for any of the gingerbread entries.

⑧ Edible decorations are encouraged and will be awarded points during the judging. Non-edible decorations are accepted, but points may be deducted if large amounts are included.

⑨ All entries must have a card attached to the underside of the base that includes the name, address, and phone number of the contestant, as well as the category that is being entered. Bases for the gingerbread projects must not exceed 24" x 24".

⑩ Entries will be judged on imagination, construction, uniformity in baking, and overall design and decoration.

⑪ The Farm Museum reserves the right to photograph entries for promotional purposes.

Categories

Heartwarming Gingerbread Houses

From Hansel and Gretel's cookie and candy cottage to Santa's snowy abode, if it's a gingerbread house that sweetens your imagination, this is the category for you. Other examples of homes in this category include Swiss chalets, farmhouses, town houses, and log cabins.

Beautiful Gingerbread Buildings

Christmas churches, firehouses, schoolhouses, stores, and other buildings that are not homes belong in this category. Any animal houses (like barns, birdhouses, and doghouses) go here as well.

Other Gingerbread Originals

Gingerbread projects that are not buildings are entered here. Examples include gingerbread trains, carousels, and baskets.

Children's Gingerbread Creations

Any projects made by persons 15 years of age and under are in this category.

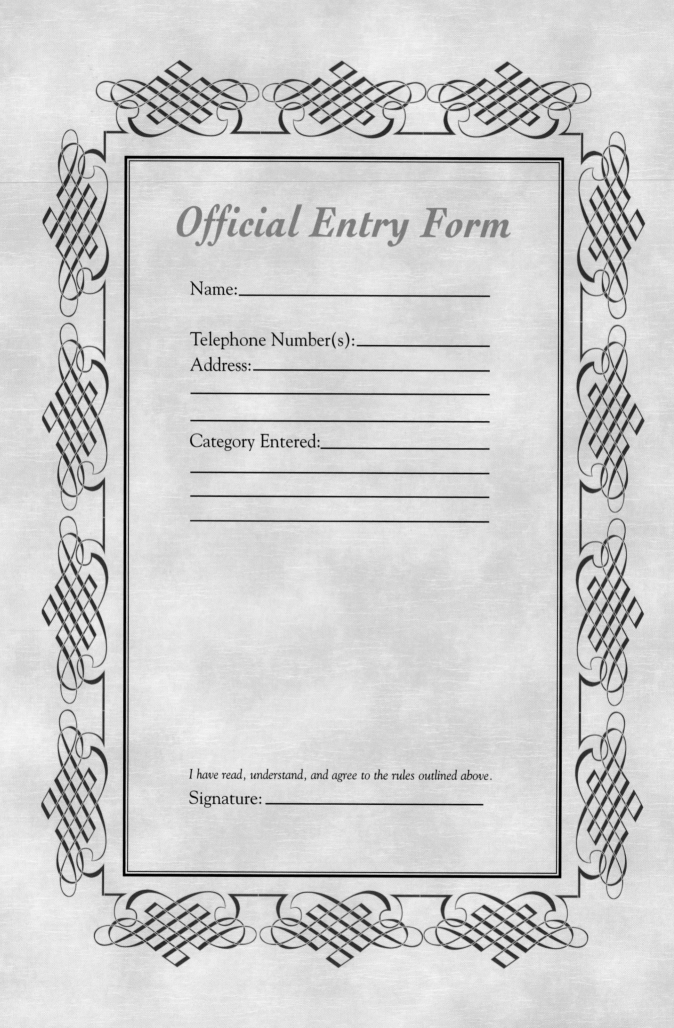

Official Entry Form

Name:_____

Telephone Number(s):_____
Address:_____
_____
_____

Category Entered:_____
_____
_____
_____

I have read, understand, and agree to the rules outlined above.
Signature:_____

How to Teach a Gingerbread Class

There are any number of places where an experienced gingerbread baker may be asked to share his or her talents by teaching a class, including schools, cake shops, senior centers, and adult education centers, to name a few. The only real requirement, besides the love of gingerbread, is a mastery of the three basic skills: baking the gingerbread, making the royal icing, and assembling the house. If you have proficiency in these areas, you have enough skill to teach a class. Just prepare your materials, plan your lessons, arm yourself with recipes and ideas to share, and you're set to go.

I have taught gingerbread classes in a number of different settings and I don't mind telling you that many years ago, before my first class, I was quite nervous. I had taught middle school for seven years, but this was to be my first experience teaching adults. I feared that I wouldn't be smooth enough in my delivery or organized enough in my methodology.

Above: Instructor Jaci Salisbury gives a student individualized instruction.

Left: A student concentrates on the task at hand.

The first thing I realized is that the teacher's personality really is not a major concern to the students. Sure they appreciate someone pleasant to listen to, but they have primarily come to learn about gingerbread. Their concern is that the teacher knows the material.

The second thing I learned is that some grown-ups are no better at listening to and following directions than 7th graders! While some classes would listen quietly and attentively, others would keep trying to work ahead before I demonstrated a particular technique. This was especially frustrating when we were assembling houses. One of the main things I try to teach students is how to apply icing and reinforce seams so that the house is super sturdy. When they worked ahead they would skip parts that would have helped them have a stronger structure. (The other two main points to my teaching are, of course, how to have a hard, crisp cookie and a stiff royal icing.) However, I would just smile as I tried to slow them down, and I always tried to keep in mind that it's just gingerbread and it's just for fun.

The following tips and guidelines should help you, too, execute fun and rewarding gingerbread classes for your students.

Each student approached his or her work differently, all with beautiful results.

Divide the class into two evenings, a week apart. The first, shorter class should run about one-and-a-half hours and consist of instruction and demonstrations. Students should bring paper and pen. The second, longer class can run three hours or more, depending on how elaborate people get with their projects. Students should bring their baked gingerbread pieces, royal icing, cake board, decorating bags, and all of their decorations.

Night One:

• Teach students how to mix the dough, roll it out, and bake it. Also show them, by demonstration, how to make royal icing. They need to see the stiff peaks for themselves to really understand what to be looking for.
• Furnish simple ideas that beginning gingerbreaders wouldn't know how to do, like making stained glass windows or ponds. Also, distribute parchment bags to the students and practice folding them together.
• Distribute a gingerbread recipe, royal icing recipe, pattern, and a supply list for the next class.

• End the class by perusing magazine articles and books about gingerbread that you have brought in.

Tip: On the second night of class, I like to provide my students with a special accessory that they might not otherwise have. It might be something purchased from a specialty shop like sheet gelatin for windows, or it could be something homemade like simple fondant shutters, "wooden" doors made with impression mats, or lace points. It can give your class that extra flair that makes it memorable!

Night Two:

• Play festive holiday music (if it's the holiday season). This really helps to set a joyful tone.
• Demonstrate how to assemble the house with liberal seam reinforcements throughout. You can either use your own gingerbread pieces or look for a volunteer who would like you to help with his or her project. (Remember to have students attach things like curtains to the insides of the windows before assembly.)
• Allow students to assemble their walls, then demonstrate attaching the roof. Begin decorating at the bottom of the roof and working toward the top.
• Circulate freely to assist students who need help building and decorating and to answer questions they may have.
• Like a host or hostess throwing a party, enjoy yourself—enthusiasm is contagious!

Auction Donations

I have always said that everyone loves gingerbread, and I proved it to myself when writing this book. When people found out about my topic, they almost always had a story to share, a person to tell me about, or a marvelous house to describe. I made many contacts this way and went to many places I wouldn't have otherwise gone. (George and I were even treated to lunch at the executive dining room of the Pentagon when we were there to photograph two gingerbread houses made for Secretary of Defense William Cohen's annual Christmas party. The gingerbread houses, made by Army chefs Petty Officer First Class Justino Abad and Staff Sergeant Kathleen Willis were highly acclaimed, festive additions to the gala.)

Given this immense popularity, gingerbread houses make excellent auction donations. The simplest way to do this, of course, is to make a gingerbread house and donate it to a charity auction. Or, if the auction is held in the off-season, you can display a picture of the proposed house to be delivered on an

Hosts David Taylor, Chuck Carr, and Jaci Salisbury.

agreed-upon date. Having the actual house present, however, will garner a higher bid.

My friend Jaci Salisbury, with her friends Chuck Carr and David Taylor, came up with an even more novel idea for a donation. They offered a Gingerbread House Raising/Champagne/Dessert Party to raise money for the Gay Men's Chorus of Washington, D.C. The first year it went for $650. The second year, after patrons found out what a smashing success it was, the same buyer had to bid almost $900 to acquire the event again.

The plan for the party proceeded as follows: Guests arrived at 7:00 p.m. and were ushered down to the cake decorating classroom in the lower level of Jaci's home. (This could be held in any room that can accommodate several large tables for decorating.) At each place setting there were all of the materials for assembling a gingerbread house: a cake board, pre-baked pieces, a decorating bag with coupler and tips, an icing knife, written instructions for future projects, and a box in which to take the houses home. Guests loaded their decorating bags with icing, and Jaci walked them through the assembly of the houses.

After the houses were put together, platters of candy and sunflower seeds were passed up and down the tables and guests had a ball decorating the houses. Few instructions were needed here; everyone had his or her own idea of what to do.

As the guests finished decorating their houses, they wandered upstairs to Jaci's dining room. There, Jaci, Chuck, and David wined and dined their visitors with champagne, cheesecake, candied nuts, biscotti, fruitcake, and more. All was served with Limoge china, crystal glassware, and linen napkins. The setting was exquisite, the food was delectable, and the party was a huge success. I can only wonder how much this unique event will go for at next year's charity benefit.

While most of us are unable to sponsor an event of such high caliber, it can serve to spark our imaginations. Maybe you could skip the reception portion or perhaps use paper plates instead of fine china. The important thing here is to get your creative juices flowing and parlay your talents in the field of gingerbread into an original and desirable auction donation.

Taking the Show on the Road to Schools and Nursing Homes

Sharing the joy of holiday house decorating with groups of children and/or senior citizens is a rewarding experience. It takes a bit of preparation on the part of the person sponsoring the event, but the joy it brings is worth the effort.

 Tip: See Graham Cracker Cottages, page 40.

Each decorating party will be as unique as the group participating, but I have learned a few things over the years:
• One house may be at each place setting, but don't hand out decorating supplies until you are ready for them to begin. The urge to create is simply irresistible!
• Warm up the group and focus their atten-

Jaci shows her guests how to load an icing bag.

Guests get down to the serious business of decorating.

Upstairs, a festive dessert party awaits.

Mothers at St. Thomas Parish Day School in Owings Mills, Maryland, are as interested in the project as the children are.

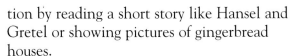
Above and right: First grade mothers at Roland Park Country School in Baltimore, Maryland, prepare graham cracker cottages for the entire Lower School.

tion by reading a short story like Hansel and Gretel or showing pictures of gingerbread houses.

• Briefly explain how to hold a decorating bag, spread icing in a back and forth motion, and decorate the roof from the bottom up. Techniques that seem obvious to experienced decorators can be quite foreign to the uninitiated.

• Distribute supplies and circulate freely.

Most people will proceed pretty independently from here.

• If you are working with children, consider having a plan for those who finish early, even if it's just a word search or a page to color.

• Don't wrap the houses in plastic before sending them home. The best way to transport a house intact is to simply carry it on its plate or cake board as is.

Chapter 8

A Gingerbread Scrapbook

Many moons ago, when I first began thinking about writing a gingerbread book, I knew that I wanted to include a section of other people's creations. After all, it is something that I would like to see as a reader and a decorator myself, and I thought others would too. What I didn't realize is what an enjoyable experience it would be for me to gather photographs. I contacted friends, ran a couple of ads in the I.C.E.S. newsletter, and even did a small blind mailing to cake decorators around the country. Pictures began pouring in, but so did cards and letters. People wrote to tell me how they made their houses, for whom they made them, and how they got started in gingerbread. I delighted in going out to the mailbox every day, knowing that there would be fresh stories, photos, and ideas, all shared freely for the love of gingerbread. I treasure them all and wish I had room to share every tidbit and tale. From the humblest homes to the most magnificent masterpieces, I sincerely hope you enjoy them as much as I do.

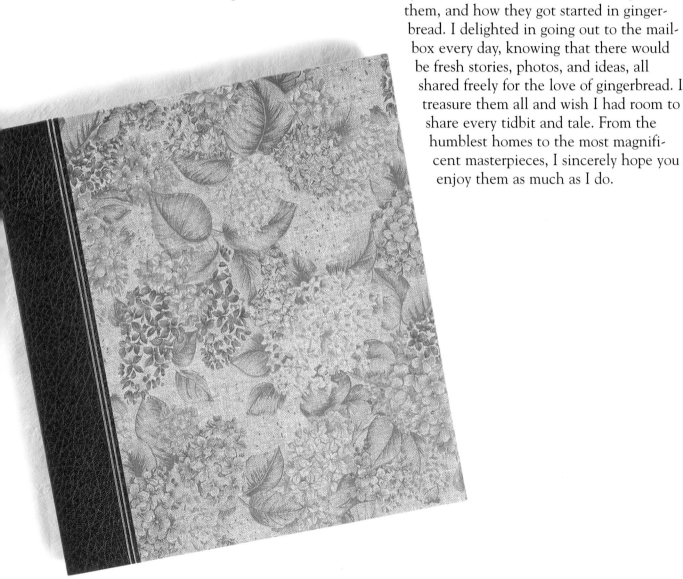

This spectacular showpiece was made by Petty Officer First Class Justino Abad for Secretary of Defense William Cohen's annual Christmas party. A view from behind shows that the decorations completely surround the house, including an icy pond.

Lisa Adam

Every positive adjective in the dictionary can be applied to these three houses: they are attractive, unique, precise, adorable, and creative. They were made by Lisa Adam of Melbourne, Australia.

The Hunt Club of Maryland was re-created down to the last perfect detail by Susan Busan of Reisterstown, Maryland.

Jillian R. Cole from Wilts, England, made this enchanting house. It's based on the style of timber and plaster cottages built in England in the 1600s.

Pat Ditmer of Albuquerque, New Mexico, created this lovely little cottage. Note the clever Fruit Stripe fence around the perimeter of the board.

Mary Beth Enderson

Mary Beth Enderson of Hampton, Virginia, doesn't make gingerbread houses—she makes gingerbread stadiums, riverboats, trucks, cathedrals, malls, towns, and more! These pictures are worth more than their combined sum of ten thousand words—they're price-less.

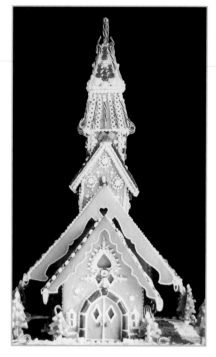

More marvels from Mary Beth, mother of eight, and grandmother of fourteen (so far!).

After entering her gingerbread creations in contests, Mary Beth often donates them to charity. Other creations go directly to charity. She is well-known in her area for the generous ways she shares her gifts and talents.

Warm, charming, and classic all describe this sweet gingerbread house made by Beverly Feather of Burton, Michigan.

It will come as no surprise that the designer of the phenomenal gingerbread houses on pages 153-157, Scott Ferguson of Tulsa, Oklahoma, is a professional architect by day. He is also an expert mold maker. If he can't find a ready-made gumpaste mold in the design he's looking for, he makes his own!

In addition to gracing the pages of this book, Scott's gingerbread houses have also been featured in Elegant Bride, Arts & Crafts, *and* American Cake Decorating Magazine.

Scott modeled this romantic piece, titled "Snow Cottage," after a David Winters miniature of the same name. The lights are a string of Grain-of-wheat lamps available for miniature snow villages. He attached them to the base of the tree before adding the boughs and snow.

Sharon Freisinger

No one re-creates the Southwest better than Sharon Freisinger of The Specialty Shop in Albuquerque, New Mexico. Like the climate these beautiful buildings represent, they truly warm the heart.

Each Christmas season for the past fifteen years, Sharon has filled the six bay windows in her shop with gingerbread displays. One of them always features baby Jesus, and another a Southwestern theme, like those shown here and on the following page. Pictured above is a fantastic replica of the Taos Indian Pueblo in Taos, New Mexico.

Salyna Gracie of Carlton, Washington, used cookie cutters in clever ways in her gingerbread work. The open doors are endearingly inviting as well.

This outstanding red Victorian was made by Jan Harris of Columbia, Tennessee. To achieve the brilliant colors, Jan added red food color to the wall dough, green to the roof, and Wilton white to the window trim, window boxes, and porch. Not surprisingly, it took Best of Show at a charity competition—and Jan won a trip for two to Miami!

"The Gingerbread Lady" of Carroll County, Maryland, D. Susan Koch, made this delightful house. Note the clever use of color flow to make the roof, windows, shutters, and doors.

Deborah Lang of Fox Chase Manor, Pennsylvania, modeled this beautiful gingerbread house after her own home. Note the three different types of trees in the yard: three-dimensional, royal icing, and rosemary.

Can you believe that this precious little house was Marci Meyerhardt's first attempt at a gingerbread house? Marci, of Springfield, New Jersey, definitely has a future in this craft!

Good ideas span the bridge of time, as this Christmas card shows. Decorator Jo Ann Nuetzel and her husband, from Baltimore, Maryland, sent out this adorable card in 1980.

Happy Holidays, 1980
The Nuetzels

Monika Paradi of Ontario, Canada, is the decorator behind the well-designed and perfectly executed pieces on pages 167-169.

More of Monika's imaginative creations.

Monika's lovely castle at left was made in ginger-bread, then covered with Choco-Pan chocolate fondant for a Chocolate Fantasy show.

This adorable A-frame hails all the way from Anchorage, Alaska. It was made by Donna Ross.

Gayla Russell of Urbandale, Iowa, has made so many fabulous gingerbread creations that it was almost impossible to choose among them. She has a wonderful way of not over-decorating so that her perfectly, evenly browned gingerbread speaks for itself. Look carefully at this photo; angels are hovering around the home of the McCaughey's, the family with the world's first surviving septuplets.

FAMILY COUNSELING CENTER
GINGERBREAD HOUSE CONTEST '94
1st PLACE AMATEUR DIVISION
NOVEMBER 19, 1994
FAMILIES MATTER!

"Adam's Ville"
...munity that Loves
Children:

Gayla has been making gingerbread and winning awards since the early '70s.

The unity of decoration and design on this lighthouse and lighthouse keeper's cottage helped it earn a first place ribbon for talented designer Deborah Campbell Ryan of Barrington Hills, Illinois.

Susan Stefancik of Mogadore, Ohio, made these three award-winning gingerbread houses. Each one has something special about it: the precious penguins of the house above, the perfect nut chimney and realistic rock wall of the house below, and the crosshatch windows and overall design of the house on the right.

Jennifer Van Scoter, Teno West, and Cynthia and Patrick Brennan

A recent trip to India inspired this masterpiece by Jennifer Van Scoter, Teno West, and Cynthia and Patrick Brennan, all of New York City.

One customer comes back year after year to Fay Shanholtzer's shop in Bakersfield, California, to order multiple gingerbread houses to give as Christmas gifts. With gorgeous Victorians like these two by designer Michelle Williams, it's easy to see why!

Staff Sergeant Kathleen Willis made a smaller, but equally endearing, ginger-bread house than Justino Abad's (see page 143) for Secretary of Defense William Cohen's annual Christmas party. The close-up shows the handiwork that went into each perfect little brick.

This priceless cottage, made by Marion Wolfe of Arlington, Virginia, shows the three bears leaving by the front door while Goldilocks is entering through the back.

Chapter 9

Still More Ideas

Have you made all of the houses in this book and now want to try something new? Or, are you looking for a fresh idea to design yourself? Here are some ideas that aren't described in detail, but are worth a try:

Beehive
Covered bridge (ala *The Bridges of Madison County*)
Covered wagon
Doghouse
Fire station
Flower pot (Grease a new clay pot, then cover with gingerbread and bake.)
Fort from the Old West
Geodesic dome
Grandfather clock (One talented decorator in Pennsylvania entered a working grandfather clock in Peddler's Village's annual contest.)
Igloo
Kennel
L'arc de Triomphe
Mayan temple
McDonald's restaurant (My next-door neighbor won second place in a local competition with this idea. She even had Santa going thorough the drive-thru on his sleigh!)
Native American tipi
Pagoda
Shoe, for the little old lady with so many children
Skyscraper
Space station (Use a lot of luster dust for a metallic, futuristic look.)
Tent with a campfire and a line of laundry strung between trees
Toy shop or Santa's workshop, with a window full of toys
Your place of employment

Also consider these ideas which have been made on a number of occasions, but which bear repeating:

Barn
Carousel
Lighthouse
Manger scene
Noah's Ark
Woodsman's cabin (The reason I didn't put one of these in this book is that I love Teresa Layman and Barbara Morgenroth's so much in *Gingerbread: Things to Make and Bake*, that I just wanted to make the same one!)

If you plan on designing your own gingerbread creation, you may want to construct the pattern out of inexpensive file folders (see the next page for an explanation).

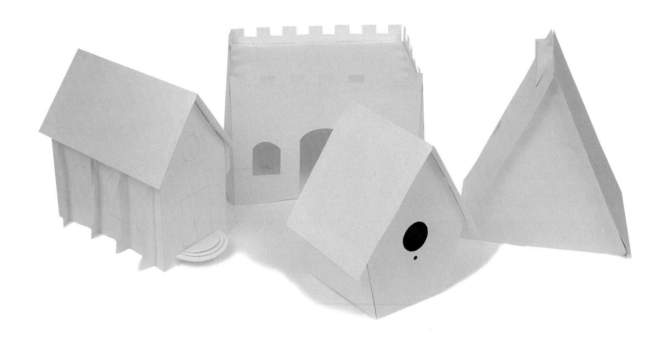

These are models of a few of the gingerbread houses from Chapter 4. Each was made out of file folders and pieced together when the houses were designed. These helped me work out the quirks of each house before I actually baked any gingerbread. Many gingerbreaders make a pattern in this manner when they are designing a house, then assemble it to make sure it actually works. You may find that what looked good on paper needs to be modified before it can be assembled in gingerbread.

Glossary

CAKE BOARD: Any board that supports a cake, but often refers to cardboard cake circles available at cake decorating stores.

CAKE DRUMS: Thick, round cake boards, available in silver or gold foil, that are able to support heavy weights and are, therefore, ideal for gingerbread houses. Most of the gingerbread houses in Chapter 4 were assembled on cake drums.

COLOR FLOW: A decorating technique in which royal icing is thinned with water and then piped into hard royal icing outlines. It is similar to coloring in a coloring book, except with icing. When dry, color flow produces hard icing pieces that can be attached to gingerbread houses or stand up when propped in icing. Also known as run sugar.

COUPLER: A screw and nut-like device that enables a decorator to change tips without changing decorating bags. The large part of the coupler is inserted into the end of the decorating bag and the tip is screwed onto the outside of the bag with the coupler's ring.

DECORATING BAGS: Cone-shaped bags from which decorators pipe icing. They are available in reusable plastic, disposable plastic, and fold-it-yourself parchment paper. Also called icing bags.

DRAGEES: Metallic-looking cake decorations (often small silver balls) that the USDA recommends be removed from food before consumption.

FONDANT: A smooth, pliable icing that is often used to cover cakes. In gingerbread it is often used, like gumpaste, to make house accessories and, like marzipan, to model figurines. Over time, fondant dries hard.

GARRETT FRILL CUTTER: A special tool used for cutting gumpaste flowers. It can be used to make lovely ruffled edges on gingerbread and gingerbread decorations, such as fondant.

GUMPASTE: A pliable, edible modeling material that can be rolled quite thin and is similar to porcelain when dry. In gingerbread it is often used to make house accessories such as shingles, shutters, and doors. In cake decorating it is often used to make realistic flowers and bows. Also known as sugarpaste.

MARZIPAN: An edible paste made from a mixture of ground almonds and sugar. In gingerbread it is primarily used for modeling figures, but it is used as a covering for cakes and as an undercoating for cakes beneath royal icing or gumpaste, especially in Europe.

Meringue powder: A dried egg white powder that substitutes for fresh egg whites in royal icing to eliminate the possibility of salmonella poisoning.

PASTE COLORS: Thick, pasty food colors preferred by decorators because they do not add a noticeable amount of liquid to a recipe. They are available in a rainbow of beautiful colors.

PIPING: The act of squeezing icing through a decorating bag to make designs and decorations or to combine pieces of gingerbread.

PIPING GEL: A clear, edible gel that adds elasticity to royal icing. In gingerbread it is most often tinted with blue food coloring to make ponds, whereas in cake decorating it is often added to royal icing when doing stringwork.

ROYAL ICING: Decorative white icing, made with powdered sugar and dried egg whites (meringue powder), that dries very hard. It is used as "cement" in gingerbread house construction, as well as to make details on houses and cookies.

SCORING: The act of cutting an outline into gingerbread rather than cutting out the entire door, window, or other opening.

TIPS: Small metal or plastic cones that have cuts in the ends to produce various shapes and designs when icing is pushed through them. They are used with decorating bags, either alone or with couplers. Also known as tubes.

Resources

American Cake Decorating Magazine
P.O. Box 22604
Kansas City, MO 64113-0604
Phone: 816-333-2800
Fax: 816-822-1320
Toll-free for subscriptions: 888-CAKEMAG
E-mail: bobharte@cakemag.com
Website: www.cakemag.com

American Cake Decorating Magazine is a full-color, full-featured bimonthly publication dedicated to American styles and personalities in all aspects of cake decorating. Each issue includes a basic skill, such as decorative piping techniques, as well as step-by-step projects, hints, recipes, patterns where applicable, book reviews, and fun stories. Write, call, or visit their website for subscription and back-issue information. A one-year subscription is currently $18.95.

Artistry With Cake—School of Sugar Art
647 F Street, NE
Washington, DC 20002-5217
Phone: 202-544-1917 or 202-544-7300
E-mail: cakedesigner@mindspring.com

Artistry With Cake is a school of sugar art run by expert decorator Jaci Salisbury. Classes and full-day workshops are offered in gingerbread, gumpaste, fondant, and more. Call or write for a free brochure.

Beryl's Cake Decorating and Pastry Supplies
P.O. Box 1584
N. Springfield, VA 22151-0584
Phone: 800-488-2749 or 703-256-6951
Fax: 703-750-3779
Espanol: 800-246-3433
E-mail: beryls@beryls.com
Website: www.beryls.com

Beryl's offers a wide variety of colours, sheet gelatin, gold, silver, and multi-colored dragees, cutters, tools, and books. A 350-plus page catalogue is available for $5, refundable with the first order.

Country Kitchen SweetArt, Inc.
3225 Wells Street
Fort Wayne, IN 46808
Phone: 219-482-4835
E-mail: cntryktch@aol.com
Website: www.countrykitchensa.com

Country Kitchen SweetArt, Inc. carries a full line of gingerbread house tools and decorations, including candy molds for making accessories out of sugar or chocolate, edible sprinkles and confections of many shapes, gingerbread pieces, gingerbread house molds, royal icing mix, sugar character lay-ons and decorations, piping gel, confectioners glaze, a huge assortment of cookie cutters, edible glitter, and much more! Send $5 for the beautiful catalogue/idea book or call with a charge card.

Designer Molds by Beatrice Knapik
3 Crestview Lane
Sutton, MA 01590
Phone: 508-865-2755

Designer Molds is the source for silicone molds reproduced from original antique molds for all sugar art. Write for a $3 catalogue (refundable with order).

Hygo Products
P.O. Box 267
Lyndhurst, NJ 07071
Phone: 877-289-4946
Website: www.hygo.com

Hygo Products is the manufacturer of convenient, hygienic, and disposable pastry bags that come in an easy-to-use roll. Contact them directly for purchasing information.

International Cake Exploration Societe (I.C.E.S.)
Membership Coordinator: Gayle McMillan
4883 Camellia Lane
Bossier City, LA 71111-5424
E-mail: gvmcmillan@aol.com
Website: www.ices.org

I.C.E.S. is an international organization devoted to the art of sugarcraft, including cake decorating, candy making, gingerbread, and more. Members not only enjoy privileges at the national level, including a monthly newsletter, but are automatically connected with a local group as well. Each year an international convention is held for all I.C.E.S. members to attend workshops, share decorating techniques, and make friends. Contact the membership coordinator for more information.

The International Sugar Art Collection
6060 McDonough Drive N.W.
Suite D
Norcross, GA 30093-1230
Phone: 800-662-8925 or 770-453-9449
Fax: 770-448-9046
E-mail: NickLodge1@aol.com

The International Sugar Art Collection by Nicholas Lodge carries a large assortment of cake decorating tools and equipment like dusting powders, palette knives, cutters, including Christmas trees, mini holly leaves, frill cutters, strip cutters, impression mats, and CelShapes molds. It also offers cake decorating classes taught by master cake decorator Nicholas Lodge. Call for a catalogue.

The Luce Corporation
336 Putnam Avenue
P.O. Box 4124
Hamden, CT 06514
Phone: 203-787-0281

The Luce Corporation is the source for Blue Magic Crystals to keep your gingerbread creations at their freshest. Call or write for descriptive literature and an order form.

Riesterer's Bakery
282 Hempstead Avenue
West Hempstead, NY 11552
Phone: 800-4-RIESTERER or 516-481-7636
Fax: 516-481-7686

Riesterer's Bakery offers cases of both large and small pre-baked gingerbread houses, as well as a complete line of royal icing and gumpaste flowers. Call or write for more information.

Sugarcraft, Inc.
1143 S. Erie Boulevard
Hamilton, OH 45011
Phone: 513-896-7089
Fax: 800-289-5552
Website: www.sugarcraft.com

Sugarcraft carries a complete line of cake decorating, baking, and candy making supplies. Also visit Sugarcraft President Dolores McCann's website at the above address where she has a section on gingerbread houses with photos and patterns.

Sweet Celebrations
P.O. Box 39426
Edina, MN 55439
Phone: 800-328-6722
E-mail: sweetcel@maidofscandinavia.com
Website: www.sweetc.com

Sweet Celebrations offers a wide variety of gingerbread baking supplies including molds, kits, books, and cutters. There are also hundreds of gingerbread accessories such as royal icing mix, icing and sugar decorations, candy wafers for shingles, candy pebbles and seashells, sheet gelatin for windows, piping gel for ice, edible glitter for snow, egg white powder, meringue powder, and gold and silver dragees. Write, call, or visit their website for a free catalogue.

Winbeckler Enterprises
16849 S.E. 240th Street
Kent, WA 98042-5276
Phone: 253-639-3544
Fax: 253-639-3308
E-mail: info@winbeckler.com
Website: www.winbeckler.com

Winbeckler Enterprises is a source for cake decorating and candy making supplies to assist you in your gingerbread decorating. They offer many items including meringue powder, royal icing mix, books, assorted holiday sugar lay-ons, and gold and silver dragees. They are also a source for pre-baked gingerbread houses, sleighs, and trains ready for assembly and decorating. Accessories and candy molds are available to decorate gingerbread for many holidays or themes. Contact them to request a free catalogue.

Related Books

Cake Styling by Nicholas Lodge and Graham Tann. London: Charles Letts & Company Limited. 1991.

A world-renowned cake decorator and leading professional photographer join forces in this guide to presenting and photographing cakes. Their numerous suggestions can also be applied to gingerbread houses, including how skillful lighting, careful positioning, well-selected props, and imaginative settings can enhance your creations and show them to their best advantage.

The Gingerbread Book by Allen D. Bragdon. South Yarmouth, Massachusetts: Bragdon Publishers, Inc. 1985.

For those who want to go beyond gingerbread houses, this book covers gingerbread boxes, eggs, cookies on sticks, marionettes, chess sets, and Chinese checkerboards. It has a variety of gingerbread recipes and clever houses as well.

The Gingerbread Book by Steven Stellingwerf. London: Charles Letts & Company Limited. 1991.

Although this gorgeous volume is out of print, it is worth the effort to find it in a library or used book store. Beautiful enough to be considered a coffee-table book, it contains such gingerbread projects as a woven basket, cookie bowl, jack-in-the-box, country church, carousel, treasure chest, gazebo, and much more.

Gingerbread for All Seasons by Teresa Layman. New York: Harry N. Abrams, Inc. 1997.

Gorgeous, full-color photographs show a dazzling array of advanced gingerbread projects for any time of year, including a baby carriage, lighthouse, Nantucket Cottage, toy shop, and Mr. MacGregor's garden, among others.

Gingerbread: Things to Make and Bake. Teresa Layman and Barbara Morgenroth. New York: Harry N. Abrams, Inc. 1992.

Gingerbread expert Teresa Layman teams up with Barbara Morgenroth to create such wonderful works of art as a woodsman's cabin, ski chalet, country store, barn, sweet shop, and more. The projects are beautiful, but fairly advanced in level of difficulty.

The International School of Sugarcraft, Book One: Beginners by Nicholas Lodge and Janice Murfitt. London: Merehurst Limited. 1988.

Arranged in a twenty-one lesson course, this book teaches many sugarart basics such as fondant, sugarpaste (called gumpaste in America), sugar molding, runout (called color flow in America), piped designs, and modeling. Encyclopedic in scope, it is a wonderfully useful addition to any food crafter's library.

Lace and Filigree by Nicholas Lodge. London: Merehurst Limited. 1992.

This beautiful book gives excellent step-by-step instructions for producing fine lace and delicate filigree in royal icing, buttercream, and chocolate. It includes designs and lace patterns that can be copied at home.

Marzipan by Pat Ashby. London: Merehurst Limited. 1986.

This charming book covers the many uses of marzipan, including flat decorations, inlays, and cake coverings. The longest section, and of the most interest to gingerbreaders, consists of fabulous pictures and instructions for figure modeling.

Rose's Christmas Cookies by Rose Levy Beranbaum. New York: William Morrow and Company. 1990.

This beautiful volume, by the author of *The Cake Bible*, offers advice, recipes, and photographs of dozens of different types of plain and decorated cookies. It also contains information on baking, storing, and sending cookies and provides pictures and instructions for creating the Notre Dame Cathedral in gingerbread!

The Wilton Way of Cake Decorating, Volume 1 edited by Eugene T. and Marilynn C. Sullivan. Woodridge, Illinois: Wilton Enterprises, Inc. 1974.

The first book in the renowned Wilton series covers cake decorators' tools, icing, color, decorating bags, basic borders, advanced borders, flower making, color flow, sugar molds, marzipan, and figure piping.

The Wilton Way of Cake Decorating, Volume 2 edited by Eugene T. and Marilynn C. Sullivan. Woodridge, Illinois: Wilton Enterprises, Inc. 1977.

The second book in the series covers flower making, roses, decorating with plain tips, chocolate, gumpaste flowers and figures, pulled sugar, candy making, and wafer paper.

The Wilton Way of Cake Decorating, Volume 3 edited by Eugene T. and Marilynn C. Sullivan. Woodridge, Illinois: Wilton Enterprises, Inc. 1979.

The third book in the series covers all of the decorating tips (tubes), including the petal, plain round, star, leaf, ribbon, giant, and specialty tubes.

Index